AN OKLAHOMA
SOLDIER

THE BERT BROOKS SR. FAMILY

Gwendolen Gael Orr Brooks is sitting. Gwen's eldest daughter Phyllis is standing with her arm around younger sister Betty. The young man is Bert Brooks, Jr. Baby daughter Mary Jane is holding her mother's hand.

AN OKLAHOMA SOLDIER

◆

A RIDE IN ONE MAN'S SADDLE

Barbara L. Nielsen

iUniverse, Inc.
New York Lincoln Shanghai

AN OKLAHOMA SOLDIER
A RIDE IN ONE MAN'S SADDLE

iUniverse books may be ordered through booksellers or by contacting:

iUniverse
2021 Pine Lake Road, Suite 100
Lincoln, NE 68512
www.iuniverse.com
1-800-Authors (1-800-288-4677)

ISBN-13: 978-0-595-35044-5 (pbk)
ISBN-13: 978-0-595-79750-9 (ebk)
ISBN-10: 0-595-35044-5 (pbk)
ISBN-10: 0-595-79750-4 (ebk)

Printed in the United States of America

As remembered, edited, fictionalized, interpreted, and dedicated with all best intentions for his descencdents by his daughter Barbara L. Nielsen.

The cover page is my father Bert Brooks, Jr., riding one of his horses, Tinkerbell, with the Saddle and Sirloin Club in an American Royal parade in Kansas City. Riding with these friends and those of the Roundup Riders of the Rocky Mountains gave him great pleasure.

Bert Brooks Jr.

To me, genealogy should be more than a record of births, marriages, and deaths. Stories and tales are needed. These are tales of my family. The births, marriages, and dates are recorded at the end of these stories.

My daughter Barbara has edited and rewritten some typed pages I composed during my retirement years when my wife and I wintered in Brownsville, Texas and summered in Windsor, Missouri and Leawood, Kansas. Barbara has been my "ghost" writer, trying to capture the "spirit" of my life, organizing the stories, inserting pictures, and adding small fictionalizations.

Contents

1

MY LIFE: HOW TO DO IT THE HARD WAY

One short sleep passed, we wake eternally,
And death shall be no more: death, thou shalt die.

—John Donne (1572–1631)

When I was in my early sixties, just after my retirement from the Marley Company, an air-cooling tower industry in Kansas City, I used to sit in my aluminum fishing boat on one of a series of five strip pit ponds my wife Mary Bob and I owned in Windsor, Missouri. The boat's motor would lazily hum and the glassy waters would reflect the varied greens of the oaks and elms surrounding the pit. Watching the orange sun slowly sinking in the west, I would think, "Heaven could be like this." The pink and the blue of the evening's first clouds would enfold the sky, and tiny breezes would caress my cheeks, dispelling the humid Missouri heat, leaving me calm and confident. Then I was cradled in precious arms.

But now my time is no longer maternal or comforting. Now time whirls callously like the black tornado that once swept through my farmyard and carried away my dear colts, Dee Day and Sunny Star, mangling their warm, furry realities, beating them with fence poles and driving green cornstalks into their squealing deformities. I have time to rest now, but the things I want to do are no longer simple.

My life has become a big front porch, but my chair no longer rocks soothingly; instead it creaks on failing, splintered boards. I am captured in a day to day struggle to carry plastic grocery bags one at a time into my soundless condominium, to open lonely soup cans, to get a wobbling spoon to my mouth. My complaining joints often make the visits of my children and grandchildren seem loud and intrusive. I concentrate too much on misery and messes, rather than on fishing and fantasies. My world is dimming, my sun sinking in darkness.

In junior high school, I wrote an essay on euthanasia. I believed in it. I wrote about the Eskimos, who when their people got old or could no longer contribute to the tribe, took them out on the ice with a little food and their bedding and left them to freeze. The survival of the tribe was more important. Now, in America, the "tribe" is large and the elderly are offered Medicare, Social Security, Meals on Wheels, Assisted Living, and Retirement Centers. When health and identity are gone, seniors live on little societal icebergs set up to maintain their lives until all bodily functions refuse to cooperate.

I would like to capture who I was, before I no longer can. I just read a book by a man whose father came back from the Korean war. His father tells a story of a moonlit night when he held one of those "yeller guys," under the chilling waters of a black, ice-laden river in a life-death struggle until the man sank. At times, I too am flooded with war memories. Mine are from an earlier war, but I have silences in my soul, silences which may have taken some home tolls. Soul wounds can ooze pus for years. I hope I have not let my past lay claims on other's futures. Yet I fear that that lives overlap lives as children emulate their parents.

Today I am in the dialysis unit watching the fluids flow in and out, currents in the stream that has carried me to this final coastal cataract before I plunge into the sea, merging my waters with all else. I drift into the past, seeking those who most branded me and those I may have seared also. Soon my loved ones will be left to offer my final reviews; they may vow to do better than I. I hope to proffer them a bud of understanding of my life, knowing I can never portray the full blossom with all its thorns and fragrances.

Left: My daughter Barbara Lu is pointing, my mother Gwen is sitting, and my grandmother Katie is standing behind them on June 17, 1945. Germany has surrendered, but the Allies are still in the Pacific.

Above: My mother Gwen is holding my daughter Phyllis, and my grandmother Katie Vashti Dunham Orr is sitting by my eldest Barbara Lu. Phyllis was born November 8, 1948 and Katie died February 15, 1952. She enjoyed seeing her great grandchildren.

2

FADING MOVIES FROM A FAILING MIND

I'm a Sooner born,
And a Sooner bred,
And when I die
I'll be Sooner dead

—University of Oklahoma Fight Song

My mother, Gwendolen Gael Orr, was born in Wheeling, Missouri, Living-ston County, on February 9, 1891; her people would soon find themselves in Red Rock, Oklahoma, and later Frederick, Oklahoma, settlers of the 160 acre free land homesteads offered from 1889 to 1907 by the Federal Government to pioneers when the Unassigned Lands were opened in five separate land runs. Her family was part of the Boomer Sooner movement, settling among Cherokee Indian neighbors. As my body shuts down, my mind reaches for her love, words, and touch, those soft, warm towels to welcome me from the cold baths of life. My mind begins to relive the stories she told me of her life.

"Gwen, come in here right now and you too, Richard Orr. Your father wants to talk to you."

The children could smell their offense, literally permeating the living area of the big, white house in Perry, Oklahoma. They should have listened, but the tiny skunks had been so enticing that the brother and sister couldn't leave them alone. They had watched their old hound Belle shake the mother to death, dividing pungent perfume among all as punishment and farewell. After Belle had exuber-antly performed the predator's role, she found her reward was not a black and white affirmation of her thoroughness, but merely a gray, cloying stench of disapproval. Her two buddies, Gwen and Richard (Dickie), had scolded her and plucked the mewling orphans from their rapidly cooling nest.

"Let's take them to the house and make them pets," declared Dickie, the lanky younger brother. Gwen stroked one tiny body as she held it in her hand. She wondered how she could drip sustenance into the bright pink mouth. She eyed the black and white Holstein cow's udder and pondered if the family's source of nourishment could be shared with these black and white species of the rodent family. She thought about the calico cat's litter that was hidden under the front porch. Would Millie adopt these three tykes or would she think them a meal of some new mouse form? Gwen was a thinker, a provider, a woman of conviction, even at eight. Yet she knew choices often could lead to disappointing conclusions.

The reception of the new additions at the house was unenthusiastic. The children's home was tense already, laden with disagreements between their mother and Stepdaddy. "Take them back to where you found them, and your father will take care of them later," rebuked Katie Vashti Orr, their mother. Gwen knew what "take care of" meant. She had seen what happened to excess kittens and puppies. She bundled them up, but failed to follow orders. Desperately hunting for a place on the entry porch she could hide them, she placed them in Stepdaddy's overcoat pocket, shushing Dickie. "We need time to think," she explained. Gwen knew better than to beg and wheedle when their mother's mouth set itself into a thin, stern line, but she also knew that sometimes Mama would give in. She and Dickie just needed to behave exemplarily now.

The children hurried to get the eggs their mother had sent them after when Belle had caught the mother skunk, just leaving the nest. Later, when Gwen and Dickie entered the enclosed porch area of the house, they were laughing and pushing each other, but carefully avoiding any collisions with their baskets of fragile, oval cargo. Then they noted the long, wool overcoat with the intended "pets" was no longer on the rack. "Where is Stepdaddy?" squealed Gwen.

"It's time for dinner now," answered Mama. "Run along and pump some water in the bowl and wash up." Gwen and Dickie's eyes locked as fear's steel links bound them. They felt assured of swift punishment from Stepdaddy as they secretly called the lean, morose man their mother had married two years after their father's death from diphtheria while working as crew superintendent on the telephone lines on the road in Joplin, Missouri.

This new daddy had come to Perry, Oklahoma as a doctor and met the young widow shortly after his arrival. The young doctor was well-trained and caring, but tired of being paid with nothing but eggs, pork shoulders, beans, and promises. He wanted to go back East where life would be richer and closer to his family. But Mama did not want to move. Her family was here. The house often whispered to the children of the disharmony. Now what would Stepdaddy say when he found the little skunks cuddled and hungry in the deep cavern of his overcoat?

It was two hours later when the two children heard the wagon wheels enter the yard. Mama sent Dickie out to help Stepdaddy stable the large bay mare Stepdaddy had purchased for his fine, black, doctor's carriage. Stepdaddy liked nice things, things that were hard to come by when treating sodbreakers. His desire to serve the suffering had been mightily tried in this red, dusty land. He was ready for the forested lands and the cleansing rains he had known as a child.

While waiting for Stepdaddy and Dickie to enter, Gwen silently darned the holes in some socks as Mama had shown her. She was an outside girl, "a tomboy," and had liked to help with the horses and shoot with her Papa or now with Stepdaddy when she could, but as Dickie grew older she found her place was becoming more and more a woman's role, confined to the dishes, the garden, and the mending. She squirmed in discontentment. "Darn," she murmured.

Then Stepdaddy could be heard entering. Dickie, promptly scooted from the porch to the warmth of the coal stove and gave a puzzled look to Gwen. About him floated an aroma whose origin was unmistakable. "Carl, whatever has happened?" Mama asked as she ran out to meet Stepdaddy. The children could hear Stepdaddy vaguely muttering to her, and then laughter resonated from the small entry that caught most of the dust and cold air between one set of doors and the other. Then Mama called to Dickie and Gwen. They came quickly with wide, blue eyes and tightened cheeks. Stepdaddy was laughing. He entered the main room and had them all sit at the wooden table their real daddy, a fine carpenter, had built. Mama made some coffee, pouring mostly warmed milk into the tin cups of the children, and Stepdaddy began his tale.

"I entered the community hall without noticing anything. Sam and Bud were already there, so I threw my overcoat on the pile by the heating stove and joined them. As the meeting began, people in the back of the room began to complain. Soon their eyes were watering and the rest of us began to notice. We couldn't figure out where the stench was coming from, but there was certainly a skunk lingering somewhere. After hunting around a bit and moving the chairs and tables, we decided we better leave and come back tomorrow, maybe even dig down under the meeting house. At that point, we just started to flee for fresh air. I reached in my overcoat pocket and pulled out my handkerchief to put over my nose. Those left inside just watched: one, two, three little perfume factories rolled out onto the floor. Couldn't help but laugh," Stepdaddy smiled at Dickie and

Gwen; he really tried to be a good Stepdaddy. It was just hard for an Easterner in Perry, Oklahoma, to keep giving with so many hands bare and worn.

3

NOTHING GOLD CAN STAY

Nature's first green is gold,
Her hardest hue to hold.

—Robert Frost (1874–1963)

"My daddy always said you got to be careful of skunks, Gwendolen; they look real cute in their black and white suits but sometimes they sure can leave a powerful smell," Becky pronounced solemnly. The two girls giggled. Gwen had taken a teaching position in Tonkawa, Oklahoma, just six months ago. Becky had become her best friend there.

Gwen had been an excellent student in her hometown of Perry, Oklahoma, and when the first to eighth grade teacher had to leave a neighboring one room school, Gwen had taken over the classes, although she was just starting eleventh grade. She had taught there and then two years in Tillman County when the Tonkawa teaching position came open, offering the nineteen year old a chance to make twice her salary and yet be closer to her Mama in Perry.

When Stepdaddy had gone back east, he had left Ma with the big, white house in Perry. Ma had rented out the rooms and Dick, Gwen, and Ma had catered to an extended family of customers. Now living in Tonkawa, Gwen had found not only her good friend Becky, but also a suitor.

The Tonkawa young men had quickly taken notice of the tall, slender beauty when she moved to town. One, in particular, attracted her, a Bert Brooks who had attended a military college there, graduating as the highest ranking cadet officer his senior year and who had played on the 1910 championship Tonkawa football team.

On their first date, Gwen and Bert had bantered about their "Sooner" heritage. Bert had been born on February 20, 1890 in Sumner County, Kansas, to James Richard and Della Torbutt Brooks. Bert's folks had been in one of the

Oklahoma land rushes that began in 1891, acquiring a homestead just across the Oklahoma line from Hunnewell, Kansas, where the majority of his people lived.

Bert had the Oklahoma Cherokee people's dark hair and high cheekbones. (He would sometimes hint some of their blood.) The Cherokees had trod a Trail of Tears when their people were forced to march from Kentucky to Oklahoma by government mandate. Bert Sr. seemed to carry some sorrow inside too for he was often moody and quiet—brooding and then explosive. Gwen loved his fire, his energy, his desire. He was three inches taller than she and his height made her feel small, dainty, and yielding, instead of regally commanding and spinsterish. With him, she felt protected, childish, and feminine. He presented her with a dilemma; she had found the strong male love she had wished for throughout her childhood, but her "tomboy" spirit fought the submissive role he commanded.

With her brother Richard, she had been able to shoot a squirrel out of a tree before he had even seen it. "You have to clean it now, Dickie; you lost," she would scoff. Then he would hit a pheasant their feet had startled from the dry, fall grass. "Your turn to wash up dishes after dinner, Gwennie," he would laugh. They had been great buddies, and the boarding house guests benefited greatly from their hunting plunder.

Now though when Gwen would hunt with Bert, a love they both shared, she found she needed to be more docile. She would let him show her how to sight and hold the barrel of the gun. His arms would encircle her on hunts and she would melt when he murmured, "Here Gwen, here's how we do it, little girl." The young lady who was the undisputed mistress of her classroom was an acquiescent pupil when Bert beckoned.

Last night at the community hall dance, he had spun her around and around; both of them laughing and the whole hall clapping. Around and around and around, they went and then he dipped her way down low. She almost lost consciousness as she gasped for air at her near fall. Bert laughed gaily at her terror. Later that night he proposed.

4

SPINNING THE YARNS

If thou must love me, let it be for naught
Except for love's sake only.

—Elizabeth Barrett Browning (1806–1861)

Around and around and around, Gwen's head seemed to spin, terror touching her tentatively, "Should she have done it? Should she have given him the money?" Five years had passed. She could hear their second daughter, little red-headed Betty Orr, cry, hungry for her breast that never seemed to quench Betty's thirst. Their first born, a towheaded toddler named Phyllis Katherin, patted, cuddled, and poked with sibling interest the tiny screamer who had just been born May 14, 1917, in Galveston, Texas. Gwen was so tired of traveling with the babies. She had no family to help and Bert worked long days and often partied with the road crews at night. Phyllis had been born August 2, 1913, in Muskogee, Oklahoma and now Betty in Galveston as the young couple had followed Ward Beekman Construction with Bert giving appraisals and directing the road crews.

Henry Ford's vehicles were growing quickly in popularity, and paved roads were replacing mud, dirt, and gravel. Bert, Gwen, and their daughters were back in Tonkawa right now where there was some family to help the young mother, but it sounded like Ward Beekman was ready to send them back to Texas. Bert was furious. He had given the Tonkawa council a bid for paving the city streets with brick, and they had accepted it, but his company had decided against the job. Bert was certain he could do it on his own if only he could get someone to stake him; he was ready to determine his own destiny. It was then Gwen had heard herself say, "I have some money."

The three years she had taught she had put away nearly two thirds of her salary; she had never had a lot growing up and it had been easy to do. She had always been true to her Scotch blood. Her ma would say, "Thrifty with a capital

T." The Orr family was supposedly a family named MacGregor whose three sons fought over the family inheritance so bitterly and so stingily that they had totally split the family up with one taking the surname Mac, one the surname Greg, and then her ancestoral Orr.

To let go of her nest egg left her totally at Bert's mercy. She didn't vote because he didn't believe women should; she didn't work because he felt she should be with the children. These restrictions were fine, but what worried her were the times when she had to stay home while he was on the road. Bert was good-looking and he loved to party. She had heard rumors that concerned her. Rumors she shook off. Yet if he could do this paving contract, then maybe he would stay here, closer to his parents and to her mother. She loved their help with the girls; she loved having her friends nearby. Henry Ford's model T would continue to drink Oklahoma's oil yields and excrete them as brick pavements or as new asphalt surfaces throughout the state. Surely the family's fortunes would grow and with them, and Bert's love for her.

Bert Brooks, Jr. in his short pants. His mother always commented on his moles, and called him, "Her little speckled egg."

5

THE SPECKLED EGG

So once I was myself a swinger of birches.
And so I dream of going back to be.
It's when I'm weary of considerations,
And life is too much like a pathless wood

—Robert Frost (1874–1963)

About now is when I, the author of these memoirs, come upon the scene. I was born at home to my parents Gwendolen and Bert Brooks, Sr. in Ponca City, Oklahoma, on December 23, 1919. The doctor who delivered me was going back and forth from our house to another where a little girl was born. When I enlisted right after Pearl Harbor in December 1941, I discovered the doctor had checked Female on my birth certificate. I wonder if somewhere a woman found out her sex was Male when she filed for a marriage certificate or a passport.

My dad whose name I bear as Bert Brooks Jr., was certainly successful after securing the bank loan to do the Tonkawa brick streets. Ward Beekman, his former employers, missed his skills, sought him out, and made him a partner, Ward, Beekman, and Brooks, but he left shortly after my birth and stayed on his own until he took in E.W. (Slim) Dahlgren, one of his supervisors, as a partner. Success was good for my family for a while. Mother had hired help and we moved less often. In fact, we were still in my birth house in Ponca City when my youngest sister Mary Jane was born at home February 1, 1924. My mother told me, "Bert, this baby will be yours to take care of and bring up." I had wanted a brother Bill, so this tiny doll learned to climb trees, holler, and shoot. I call her "Bill" off and on to this day.

In my family, Education was the Almighty and Male Heirs were not Cowards. I started school at age four, but had to do two years of kindergarten because only six year olds could be in first grade. Later I would skip two and one half grades and graduate from high school early. My mother was relentless in her desire for me to do well. Both my mother and father warned that if I got a spanking at school, "You will get a worse one when you get home." Both agreed too that if I got into a fight, "You better take it like a man." Men didn't cry.

Hunting was important in my family, probably as a way to get dinner when my mother and father were small, but later on as a sport both enjoyed. My father used to hunt often, including going to South Texas for white tail deer, New Mexico for mule deer, Colorado for elk, and Wyoming for antelope. He was a crack shot and always got his limit; he usually only shot trophy animals. He would come home from his trips to South Texas with a big buck tied to each front fender. One year he brought home a javalina and helped me hang its mounted head over my bed. On the wall beside my bed, I had some deer hoofs mounted, and I kept a 410 shot gun there on the upturned ankles.

Dad had killed a black bear, which was made into a rug, with the bear's head, mouth wide open, still attached to the hide. It lay in the doorway between our living room and our dining room. One of my eldest sister's (Phyllis') boyfriends gave her a Scotty dog Tyler that considered this rug its personal potty place. One day, I got under the rug and crawling on my hands and knees, backed Tyler up into a corner, swinging the bear's head back and forth toward him. He took a bite at the nose, but from then on he would skitter around that rug with fearful eyes and bark at the back door if nature called. Dad's trophies were magnificently realistic.

I got my first gun when I was eight. My birthday was two days before Christmas. When I walked into the breakfast room, I found a big box awaiting me. My blue eyes sparkled, "Is it a 410, Mom?" With all three sisters gathered round, I lifted the lid and there were the stock and trigger section of the 410 shotgun I had been promised. "But where is the barrel?" I queried. Mama just smiled, "Your Dad will be here for Christmas, and you will get the barrel then." I could hardly wait. Both my mother and father had already taught me how to stalk, wait, and sight on her 20 gauge, but now I would have my own 410!

"Treat every gun as if it is loaded, Bert," my dad would tell me, "and never point a gun at someone unless you have to use it." Children needed to know gun safety and that a 22 rifle could kill at a mile and a half, so the rifleman better know good and well what was behind his target.

Anyway, Dad had a 22 rifle on a 30.06 frame, weight and everything, and we would take it out and practice with it. He would put a little piece of paper in a log at the bottom of a bank about 100 feet away and hand me his rifle, "If you hit it the first time, Bert, I'll give you a $1.00." That was big money, but I never hit it. He would offer 75 cents the second shot, and then start knocking a nickel off for each additional shot. After I had hit it a few times; the piece of paper that was left was smaller than a dime. Then he would take the rifle and hit it the first time every time. My dad's training probably helped me survive World War II.

It was necessary to know how to shoot when I grew up. When I was about ten, Mother, a light sleeper, woke up about midnight and called out, "Who is that?" She thought one of we children were up. There was no answer. She called a little louder "Who is that?" We were all awake by then. Again she got no answer. She called out a third time louder yet, and a strange voice yelled back from the top of the hall stairs, "Wouldn't you be surprised!" We heard the man run down the stairs in the dark and fall over a chair in the living room. Shortly thereafter we heard a car speed off. I had grabbed my 410 off the wall and had come running out of my room, wondering if it were loaded or if I was just going to have to bluff. During the depression, there were a lot of hungry, homeless men who would come asking for work. My mother would try to find chores for them when she could.

Once Mrs. Dahlgren, my father's partner's wife, came by to visit my mother, and brought a couple of her boys with her. They were closer to Mary Jane's age, and Janey (Bill), decided to take them upstairs and show them the deer heads, javalina heads, and other trophies. When they were in my room, she took my 410 off the wall, not realizing it was loaded, and shot between the two boys. "Pow!" the bathroom wall was pierced before their widened eyes. I certainly failed to teach my brother "Bill" one of the cardinal rules of gun safety—to always treat a gun as if it were loaded. "Mom, Mom," the boys came running down the stairs, "Janey shot a hole in the wall." After a quick inspection of the damage, Mrs. Dahlgren and her boys somewhat haughtily departed.

6

HUNNEWELL SUMMERS

Inebriate of air am I,
And debauchee of dew,
Reeling through endless summer days,
From inns of molten blue.

—Emily Dickinson (1830–1886)

Many boyhood summers I spent at my Uncle Willis Brooks' farm southwest of Hunnewell, Kansas, to help with chores and visit my cousins. It was really my dad's farm. My grandparents had left it to both Willis and dad equally, but as was often whispered, "Uncle Willis didn't quite cut the mustard," and my dad had bought his half, but kept him and his family on, letting them have all of the crops. Dustbowl farming wasn't easy. Off and on Willis would work on one of dad's highway construction jobs.

The home on the farm was not modern, although it did have some electricity provided by a generator and storage batteries. We would go to the outhouse to relieve ourselves or use a slop jar on a cold night and then have to empty it in the morning. We had a hand pump in the kitchen that got water from a cistern. We could pump into the cistern with the outside pump, but the windmill often pumped just enough for the cattle, leaving us waterless if we had not thought ahead. Baths were on Saturday evening whether we boys thought we needed one or not. They were in a wash tub in the kitchen. We would have to chop the logs for the wood stove, and then my cousin Jack's ma Aunt Effie would heat the bath water on the wood-burning stove right after we had cleaned up the supper dishes. Jack and I were childhood friends as well as relatives.

"Come on Bert," Jack yelled. He was a year older than I, brown, assured, and muscular. My Uncle Willis let us fish and hunt a lot. We had to milk cows morning and night by hand, using a stool that looked like a "T" to sit on, but then we were often free. The cow barn including the milking shed was at the top of a cliff, which had a trail going down it and a creek at the base. There was a shallow spot there that we could cross to get to the pasture. A short distance up the creek was our swimming place where we kept a flat bottom boat. This creek and swimming hole we shared with an occasional water moccasin and turtle. Some were pretty dang big, and we certainly would move out fast when we saw any moving sticks or debris.

The day I remember Jack and I had our 22's with us, in case we saw a squirrel or a rabbit, but we were going "noodling." Our favorite swimming area was about a mile up the road from Uncle Willis' place. In the river below the swimming hole was a rock ledge that went out into the middle of the river and had many holes in it. During June, the catfish would spawn here and we could catch them with our hands. This was called noodling. We could catch some big, old catfish by diving down to these holes at the bottom and reaching behind their heads to grab their two side fins and drag them out and up. Their silent struggles would stir the red silt dust from the bottom, painting in vivid streaks the fear of the victim and the joy of the victor. Uncle Willis had warned us, "Keep your fingers out of those big, ole, rasp mouths, or there may be more than mud painting that river water."

Jack and I were trying hard to perfect this country boy art. Uncle Willis had a story he would always tell us, "Once it rained buckets and these huge, shallow pools formed just off that creek bed there, but that lil' ole creek was still runnin' plenty good. Well, me and my brother Bert Sr. was walkin' along and I saw the biggest, ole catfish ever just a lyin' there in one o' those pools. I ran out and stuck my arm in that ole fish's gill and thrust it right out through his mouth, but that damn, ole fish clamped its gills down on my arm and started high tailing it for parts unknown. Me, I was a screaming and a blubbing along, but my brother hung onto me and we pulled ashore one 50 pound catfish that night. Me, I wasn't sure if I was the bait or the fisherman."

Tales of seventy to eighty pound catfish abounded in this country and even one of a 125 pounder that had to be drug out by horse, with a rope tied to a cottonwood tree and then run through the catfish's gills. Jack and I were sure planning to emulate catches like that sometime, but we wanted to pass up Uncle Willis' blubbing and screaming, because we were mighty hunters.

The wind was up a bit and the dust was blowing. Some of it got in my eye and I stopped to wipe it out, blinking a big, wet tear down my cheek. "Whatcha crying about, woman-cousin?" my country mentor goaded. I just turned around and decked him flat.

Whoa, was I surprised. When he sat back up, he picked up his 22 and pointed it straight at me.

He was plenty angry, "You little punk, you little coward. You little cheapshot. I'm going to blow you to bits."

I just stared at him. "Your dad will beat your butt if you shoot me, Jack," I said. We just glared at each other. But then he laughed, "You son of a gun, I can't believe you can hit like that."

I was really proud and determined not to apologize because Jack was always whacking away on me. "Come on," he smiled. "Let's celebrate." He started peeling off his jeans and in two minutes we were both skinny dipping in that little, red creek, hollering, hooting, and hopping, best friends scaring away any chance of catfish dinner. That lucky punch would start making school easier for me to handle.

Later that night, we'd catch us a couple of chickens, chop their heads off, pick them clean, and have Aunt Effie cook us some fresh fried chicken, every bit as good as those big, old catfish. We never did "let the cat out of the bag" by snitching on each other about this episode.

Another time Jack and I had saddled the cowpony we used to drive the cows to the corrals. We both rode bareback, taking turns on who sat in front. There were four work horses too, but the cowpony was part thoroughbred and had come from a circus. Today as we prepared to mount by hurling ourselves off the wooden corral posts, we were kidding each other about "cutting our feet," which meant stepping into one of the big cow piles of manure in the corral which I had just missed doing. Jack had failed to zip his pants that day and we were laughing about "his barn door being open and his horse getting away." It was the start of another great day.

Uncle Willis' hound dogs would follow us around in hopes they could tree a squirrel and have us shake it down to them. A lot of the times when we were without our rifles, we would see a squirrel up an isolated tree. We would throw rocks at it and get it excited; it would jump to the ground and the hounds would kill it. Then we would not come home empty handed, but as supper suppliers.

Today we were on a mission. We had been over by a neighbor's place and noticed a steady flight of bees always going the same direction. This morning we followed them and found this bee hive about forty feet up this enormous, old elm tree. Jack decided, "We can blow excelsior smoke into the hive; then the bees won't sting us and we can get some honey comb." It was a great idea, but there was one problem: the opening to the hive went down into the tree and the smoke went up.

Jack's next idea was to try an axe. We shinnied up the tree and tried to chop a hole into the hive about five feet below the opening; now please remember we were thirty-five feet up. That elm was tougher than rawhide and our axe just bounced off it. After half an hour, we could hardly see a chip's worth of progress.

Now came Jack's next idea—remember he was a year older and I certainly seemed a slow learner when it came to who was doing what. Jack convinced me that we could get some cheese cloth, drape it over a hat, and tuck it in at the neck; then we could put about three pairs of socks on our hands and arms and that "I", repeat "I," could reach in the hive and break off chunks of comb and drop them down to him.

Believe it or not, this plan did not work. Before I could grab anything, I discovered that the socks were not sting proof. My arm came out just covered with bees. I was forty feet up a tree and couldn't run. I just had to hang there and take it. After awhile, the bees calmed down and I slid back down. Although I had only been stung on my hand, my hand and arm were swollen clear above my elbow from the little warriors' venom. Some honeycombs are sweeter than others, but we never knew if this one had a sweet clover flavor or not. We sure did find out what a "hiding" was though when we got home. Uncle Willis saw fit to laugh, but he also saw fit to assure us that the leather strap hanging on the wall would take the skin from any young men who had such crazy "sweet tooths" again.

Later that night, Jack, I, and Wayne, my eldest cousin, were moping sadly in bed; Wayne suddenly started to laugh. "What is it, Wayne?" I blurted. "Hey, Bert, this was really a tough titty day, wasn't it?" I began to chortle, increasing the pain in my enlarged arms. In my day we had washing machines that had a set of rollers on them. A woman had to squeeze the water out of the wet clothes by inserting them into the rollers. Now if her chest got too close, that was not too good. Whoa, did Jack and I ever think that expression was a funny one when we were just boys. "Tough luck" as a saying never made us giggle so.

As a young man, I stand in front of our Oklahoma City home at 2115 N.W. 18th.

7

TOURING WITH MOTHER

Two roads diverged in a wood, and I—
I took the one less traveled by,
And that has made all the difference.

—Robert Frost (1874–1963)

When I was twelve, my family had a huge seven passenger Packard that the funeral homes all wanted to buy. My mother decided I should learn to drive, and one day after school, she said, "Bert, let's take a little ride in the country." We found a paved road with no traffic, and she put me behind the wheel. Needless to say, I felt proud. I slowly released the brake and we "putted" down the road. "Mom, what do I do when I get to that motorcycle?" "What, honey, what motorcycle?" she asked. I squinted, "Well, I think maybe it's a horse." "Bert, there is no horse." I was getting a bit panicked as the object came closer, "Well, Mom, that car, what do I do when I get to that car!!!" "Bert, are you talking about the bridge up ahead?" A whole new world opened to me after she made me an eye appointment. The doctor jokingly pronounced, "You are blind in one eye and can't see out of the other," and fitted me with the thickest, coke bottle lenses imaginable.

After the Packard, Dad gave mother a Reo touring car with wooden spoke wheels and a canvas top. I was spitless. We visited relatives a lot. No one ever worried about a lack of beds. All of the kids got blankets and slept on the floor. I remember one time visiting my cousins down by Lubbock, Texas, and one night they took us kids out and stole watermelons. We broke them open and just ate the hearts out of them. I wasn't too proud of doing that. I still am not.

My grandmother Orr still ran a boarding house in Perry, Oklahoma, and we would often visit. In those days, the roads did not run between the big cities, but from little town to little town, and to get from one big city to another, motorists had to go through all of these little towns. Most highways were not paved but were graveled, and the farm to market roads were not even graveled, but just graded up with a ditch on each side. As the roads did not run direct, the distances were much greater than they are today, maybe fifty to seventy-five percent farther. After a heavy rain, drivers would be all over the place, slipping in the mud ruts. Generally they found themselves at the mercy of a passing farmer with a team of horses to pull their cars out of a ditch. Tires were not the quality of today and a driver better be competent at changing them. Bridges were another item in short supply. My mother would cross the Cimarron River where the road met a shallow ford, but only when it had not rained and the river was down. Speed traps already existed. Passing through. Mulhall, Oklahoma, meant "Slow down" in the Brooks' motoring book.

In the late 1920's, my mother took us on several trips, which with the roads the way they were was quite a deal. To me, Amelia Earhart, the famed woman aviator of my time, and my mother had a lot in common. One year Mom took all four of us to Colorado. We went to the Garden of the Gods, drove up Pikes Peak, and went to Cripple Creek and Leadville. Some of the roads were so narrow that we could not pass an oncoming car. Several times we or the other car would back up to a wide spot so that passing was possible. Some boys kept trying to flirt with my sisters by passing us, then making us pass them. My sisters were laughing and waving.

Another summer Mother took us to New Mexico and Arizona. We rode down the Grand Canyon on mules and had a picnic. About noon it rained and the Colorado River flooded. We had a terrifying trip back up to the rim. From the Grand Canyon, we went to the petrified forest, painted desert, and on to Los Angeles. We rented a house at Santa Monica for a month close to the beach. My sister Phyllis got badly sunburnt there and was really miserable. We took the boat over to Catalina Island. Then we drove up the coast to San Francisco. It was late July or early August and we just about froze there. Then we went on up through the redwoods, driving through the tunnel that had been made in one of the trees. We went as far as Portland Oregon before heading for home.

My mother did all of this with four tired, often fighting, screaming kids in the car, and with her mother Katie, sitting alongside, but still, "backseat driving." I take my hat off to Mom. I believe that it was on this trip out west, that something went wrong with the car, and we were in a garage getting it fixed. My sister "Bill" and I were bored and messing around in the garage. We found a punch press and after finding out how it worked, I talked my sister into putting her finger under it and lowered it to where it just touched her finger; then I smiled and brought it back up. Then it was my turn to put my finger down. The problem was that "Bill" didn't understand how it worked and tromped down on the pedal. It left me with a scar in the first joint of my trigger finger on my right hand. After that I never have had any trouble remembering which is my right hand. I just look for the scar.

I am not sure whether it was on this trip, or a different one, that we went to Yellowstone and the Grand Tetons. At any rate, Mother took us there. We saw Old Faithful and several other geysers and bubbling mudpots. All over the park, the rangers warned us not to feed the bears and not to leave food in our car. Most people ignored the warnings and fed the bears, but nearly every morning when we came out we would see some car that the bears had opened up like they had a can opener because they could smell food inside. Most car tops were made of plywood and canvas then.

Anyway at Old Faithful Trading Post, I went in and bought a souvenir ash tray with a bear on it for my dad. The clerk put it in a sack and I proceeded outside. Who did I meet but one of the bears. What did she see but a boy with a nice, brown sack? What does a bear think when she sees a brown sack? Food, that's what. Well, I wasn't about to give my dad's present to that bear, so I held it as high as I could above my head. This big black bear came over, slowly, surely stood upon her hind feet, and put her paws on my shoulders. I was frozen, with the sack held straight up. She stuck her nose up, smelled the sack, and then dropped back down and lumbered off, looking for someone else with a brown bag. The Yellowstone Bear patrol was usually hungry, but friendly, until surprised or angered. It was a good thing I froze.

My mother was an independent woman; she had to be with my father gone most of the time on his road jobs. One summer, she loaded all four of us and drove us through as many Civil War battlefields as we could find. We ended up in Atlanta, Georgia. We had planned on going to Florida, but that night in Atlanta was so hot that the mattress cover faded off through the sheets onto our pajamas. We decided enough Civil War; we would go north through Washington, D.C., New York City, Boston, and into Canada, driving through Quebec and Ontario on our way back and then down through Chicago. The further north we got in the U.S. the more people would ask us, "How many Indian raids do you have out there?" They thought Oklahoma was uncivilized country.

To this day, I think of these journeys as a family. My mother was always teaching, always reassuring, and always interested.

My dad, Bert Brooks Sr., is sitting on the fender beside the tire. He loved to hunt.

8

WORKING AND FISHING WITH DAD

The world is charged with the grandeur of God.
It will flame out, like shining from shook foil;
It gathers to a greatness, like the ooze of oil
Crushed. Why do men then not reck his rod?

—Gerard Manley Hopkins (1844–1889)

My dad had partnered with a chemistry teacher Wayne Barbour and a promoter and ex-navy officer, T. A. Nicholson, to convert some undesirable oil wells with high asphalt content by Stroud, Oklahoma, to road oil. My dad supplied the money; Barbour, the idea; and Nicholson, the sales ability. When Barbour and Nicholson had approached Dad, they told my father that he could have any interest in the corporation that he wanted. He said, "There are three of us; let's split it three ways."

This startup would become Allied Materials. With the depression, Allied's President T.A. Nicholson and Vice President Wayne Barbour had to keep borrowing money. My dad and his road construction partner E.W. (Slim) Dahlgren once flipped a coin to see if they should keep on financing them. Later on, my dad would give Slim half of his stock in Allied. Slim and Dad formed many companies and liquidated them over time. Besides highways, they also built pipelines.

During this era, Dad and his partners decided they needed a Stenson airplane to meet their travel needs. A pilot was sent to bring it to them. He needed to land in Fort Worth, Texas, for fuel. Love Field in Dallas was just being built and this pilot landed in a big ditch on this new air field and wrecked the plane. After it was repaired, he brought it to Oklahoma City. Maybe the Stenson's first trip should have been taken as a warning, but it wasn't. All of the partners took flying lessons, but they always took a professional pilot along with them. One day they flew into a mountainside in New Mexico. All four of them jumped out and ran around the plane, but no one was hurt. One day they got caught in a snow storm while flying in New Mexico. They finally succeeded in setting the plane down at an emergency airport. Dad walked away and sold the plane.

In about 1937 or 1938, Allied Materials had found a little oil field down in Carter County, Oklahoma. It wound up causing the partners to having a "falling out." Part of this field had been taken in the corporate name and part of it as individuals. T.A. Nicholson was bragging all over the place about what a great oil find it was, and every one else was trying to get him to shut up. So they set a price on the corporation at which they would either buy T.A. out or he could buy them out. The choice was his. He elected to be bought out.

The oil field turned out to be highly fractured. When they started, they drilled a well, skipped a location, drilled a well, skipped, and so on. Then they came back and drilled those that they had skipped. Every one that they had skipped turned out to be a dry hole. If they had moved over one location to start with, they would probably have had nothing.

As a boy, I often worked, selling magazines, or bagging groceries. Three summers during my teens, I worked on Allied highway jobs. It was probably about the summer of 1934 that Allied built the highway from Miami to Afton, Oklahoma. Dad's company had bought the largest Caterpillar diesel bulldozers made at that time for this job. They were shipped in by flat car, and the factory sent some experts down to show the men how to operate the bulldozers. These experts couldn't get them started to get off the flat cars. The fourth day, Superintendent Bowen, who was quite a mechanic, took over. Before night, he had them running and drove them off the flat cars. Farmers and people from all over came to see these Cats. We had LeTourneau carryalls, rock plows, sheepfoot rollers, and other road equipment. I was very proud of my dad.

One morning, Slim gave me some parts, "Take my car and take these on out to the job." I drove around our construction barricade and on down the road. A guy was standing at the side of the road. He stepped out into it a little way and held his hand up. I thought, "Hmmm, some farmer hitchhiking down to see our Cats." I shook my head, "No," at him and went on. It was not too much farther to a little bridge. At that point, I remembered that the road crew had picked up a case of dynamite that morning. "Screeeech!" I hit the brakes and almost came to a dead halt. I could hear someone yelling then, "Get the Hell out of there, you crazy kid!" I swerved Slim's car in the tightest U-turn I had ever made and gunned it down the road. I made it about 200 feet when I heard the dynamite rumble and felt the bridge collapse. My hands began to tremble. I slowed the car and just sat there.

At Spiro, Oklahoma, I paid seven dollars a week for board and room. I had fried chicken every night, and the lady packed a lunch for me. Occasionally she would put cold fried chicken in it too. I helped build part of the old Highway 66 which replaced a one lane paved road from Miami to Afton, Oklahoma.

Slim, not my father, gave me my talk on "SEX" one day while he was driving me out to a summer job. His advice was good, but I am glad that I did not try all of it. He told me, "Always wash your privates off with soap and water afterwards; if there isn't soap and water, use gasoline." I guess he thought I'd always have a can of gasoline in a car or something. Well, I washed my arms with gasoline once in the refinery, and I don't think anyone wants his "parts" that clean. Slim also told me, "If you are ever in any trouble you don't want to discuss with your folks, you can talk to me, Bert." I always liked Slim; his oldest son was about three years younger than I was. Slim was probably practicing on me for his talk with his boy. At least, someone talked to me.

I worked on a highway job outside of Carlsbad, New Mexico, one summer. Allied was paving the road with asphalt. My jobs were based on my dad's theory, "Men should start at the bottom and work their way up." Every summer I got to start again at the bottom, so that I could work my way up. This summer I worked alongside Carlos, a young Mexican man. Carlos was about five years older than I was with a wife and small child. We were paid 40 cents per hour, which was the first minimum wage. A crane would take the asphalt out of a railcar and drop it into a truck box. Our job was to level the truck off with rakes. The hot asphalt would stick to our rakes and build up until our rakes got so heavy we could hardly lift them.

Superintendent Bowen was on this job too. He was about 5'9" and weighed about 225 pounds. He could start a fight and clear a bar out in a hurry. About the time, the Carlsbad job was winding up, he had to go to town to get the final papers in a divorce from what seemed like his tenth or eleventh wife. He stopped in a bar and did a little celebrating before he came back. When he arrived on site, he took over the crane to move the last of the asphalt out. Carlos and I were not too happy with the gyrations of the shovel, but we weren't going to say much to Bowen. We just kept our eyes wide open and hunkered down when that shovel came close.

My mother was not happy with the profanity I picked up during my "road" summers. But, in fact, I was quite pleased about being able to hold my own with the other men. She pointed out, "You have three sisters who do not need to hear that sort of language," and "Anyone who can't find a better way to express himself must be just plain dumb." In our home, boys and girls were different. Girls always had a set time that they had to be home. This curfew could vary if something special, such as a dance was going on, but it was still a set time. In contrast, I had no set time as long as I arrived at what seemed a reasonable hour, and no one ever seemed to quibble over what reasonable was for me; maybe that was because any girls I dated had set times to be home too. I really didn't have much to do after I took them home. All of us had to let Mother know when we got home. "So that I won't wake up and be worried that you aren't here," was what she said.

When my dad was home, he was often moody and would whip me on occasion with his belt. He would hit me until I would cry and then he would quit. The last time that he whipped me we were eating breakfast. He was reading the Oklahoma City newspaper when I came in. My mother slipped and nearly dropped the plate of bacon she was about to set on the round, wooden table that had hosted a series of events, including my circumcision in 1925. "Oh, I almost broke my neck," she laughed as she slid precariously across the floor, perhaps, on a drip of grease. I was thirteen and, thinking myself quite cute, I quipped, "Too bad you didn't." Dad threw down the paper and growled, "Go to your room, Bert. You don't speak like that to your mother." He came up to my room with a rawhide mule whip that he had picked up in Mexico. It was old and dry, and he broke the lashes off the end of it before he quit, but this time I didn't cry and he didn't whip me again.

My father had a lot at Lake Aluma Chulosa just outside of Oklahoma City. At one point, he wanted to build an adobe house out there and paint it purple. None of us wanted to live in a purple house, so the house never was built. Still I spent much time out there. The property had an eleven acre lake on it, as well as a ten acre deer pen. My dad brought out a pair of geese we had kept in our backyard in town until keeping them in town became illegal. We clipped their wings, and they attracted many more. I can remember running from these geese when they were mad. Flapping their wings and using their bills with drill force, they could be formidable adversaries when we kids had gotten their ire up.

One of the teachers at my high school, a Mr. Payton, would fish with me there. He was a professional wrestler at one time, and his eyes were fascinating. They were large and his eyelids drooped over them. He was the only teacher that I ever saw that could walk into a class room where the kids were raising hell and not say a word, but just look at the class, and they would become instantly quiet. He taught my chemistry, biology, and geology classes.

Stories of Payton's hypnotic skills circulated in our school. During her summer school classes with him, my sister Betty said he hypnotized two of the students. He told one, "Jerry, go across the street after I snap my fingers and buy everyone in the room a candy bar." Jerry did just that when he awoke from the trance. Payton reimbursed him. The other student Reed sat on the shady side of the classroom. "Reed," Payton said, "the sunlight is extremely bright in here. When I snap my fingers, you are not going to be able to sit still until the blinds are closed." Reed fidgeted after he was woken until he received permission to shut the blinds. He then shut ever blind in the room.

Payton told me that one time he was teaching in a crowded country school, which had a troublemaker named Thomas. When he got to the hypnosis section of his class, Thomas volunteered as a subject, so Payton had him recite, "Mary had a little lamb" in front of everyone. After that, Payton laughed, "I would just glance in his direction and he would settle right down."

Payton and I collected some snakes and black widow spiders for his class at my dad's lake place. In fact I came up with a fantastic source for black widow spiders. These spiders make their winter nests in black locust bean pods, which I had been collecting in my coat pockets. My collection proved quite dangerous.

Later, my father had a beautiful adobe home outside of Santa Fe, New Mexico. It was one of the showplaces. (According to my dad, it had been painted purple at one time, but had weathered. It just looked like adobe to me.) It had a fireplace in each bedroom. The living room was a two story affair with enormous logs for beams. Between the logs, branches about 4 inches in diameter were laid in a herringbone pattern. The furniture was Southwestern. There was a stair and balcony in the living room which led out onto a roof. The house was on a mountainside overlooking Santa Fe. I spent about a week at his Santa Fe home once. We had several meals at the La Fonda in the center of town. Then he took me up to El Vado Lake which was just outside of Chama. The road was gravel all the way. He had a lease on the buildings that the men constructing the dam there had previously used. When the dam was built, my dad had converted these buildings into a hotel, restaurant, and lodging. The first year that he had the place he hired a manager away from Eagle Nest Lake to run it. This man had many connections and got several people to come to El Vado. He had just one small drawback. He "had a pocket for business and a pocket for himself." He preferred the second pocket.

The next year my dad hired Frank, a hunting partner from South Texas, to run the place. This man was honest, but he had never run anything other than a filling station and didn't have the slightest idea about running a resort. For instance, he strung a clothesline in front of the nicest guest rooms and hung his long underwear to dry. The guests had to duck between Frank's flying flannels to get to their rooms.

El Vado was three miles at its widest spot and fifteen miles long. Fishing on the lake was good, but no one had ever caught many fish trolling. Dad had a lot of boats there that he wanted to rent, so Frank took me out to show me the art of trolling. "Then you can be a guide," he said. We were both rigged up with a lure someone had reportedly had a strike on. I caught a fish. We went a while, and he changed me to a different, bigger lure and took mine. I caught another fish. He immediately changed to that lure and changed me to another. I caught another fish. As it goes, I caught six fish before he caught one, and so I passed my guide test easily. I would often guide for my father's business acquaintances.

One day late in the summer, Frank, the hotel manager, had a friend come up and asked me to take the two of them fishing. Trolling was slow, so we went and tied up in some trees to fish. We all had the same lure. First Frank would catch a fish and then I would. His friend Harry Longacre didn't catch a thing. Soon Harry started this tale of another fishing trip that he and the manager had taken, "We were fishing off a dam. First I would catch a fish and then Frank would. A fellow about 150 feet away hadn't caught anything, so he laid his pole down with the line still in the water to come down and see what we were using. This guy had gotten ten or fifteen feet away from his pole, when off into the water it went with this beautiful fish dancing along ahead." Harry laughed, "Any damn fool that lays his pole down with the line in the water deserves to lose it."

He had hardly gotten the words out of his mouth, before I hooked a fish. Yep, he laid his pole down with the line still in the water and reached back for the landing net. Bingo, over the side his pole went with this magnificent fish jumping away pole, line, and sinker. I turned around to see what the commotion was about and there went my fish. We were in about nine feet of water, so I thought I could dive in and catch my line across my body and get my rod back. Well, I forgot to take my watch off and that was its last tick. Both fish and both rods became lake bait.

Speaking of fish stories, we had one hard luck angler at El Vado who seldom did any thing right. The week before he had been fly fishing and hooked a fly in his nose. He always fished in the river below the lake. This week he had hooked a 4 pound rainbow trout, a big trout in the swift river waters. He recounted, "I started to pull the fish in and the tip of my rod broke off. Then my reel got tangled, so I started hand over hand up my rod, trying to bring this trout in. I got him lodged between two boulders and my leader broke. So I jumped into the river and blocked him in. I just scooped him up and threw him on the bank. He was flopping away there, trying to get back in the water. I straddled him and held him down until he was still. Finally I got a good hold of his gills and yanked him up. All around me was this lush, green poison ivy bed!" This angler had oozing pimples of ivy pus all over his arms, face, and chest.

One day in August I was out by myself, trolling in the vicinity of the dam. Nothing was biting, except mosquitoes and flies. A bunch of my friends came down to the boat dock on the other side of the lake and went swimming. I made up my mind that I was going to add some weight to my lure and let it out trying to sink it way down. I would make one more circle and then quit and go swimming. At one point, I thought I felt a couple of tugs and set the hook, but nothing. So I decided to go swimming. I essentially stopped the boat and started reeling in. When the line was about halfway in, I thought I felt a couple of tugs, set the hook, nothing. I didn't know that I had a fish on until he was within six feet of the boat. He looked as long as my leg. I grabbed the landing net and before he had a chance to fight, I had him scooped up and in the bottom of the boat with the fish net over him. I climbed on top.

My friends were clapping and cheering. I weighed him on the meat scales in the grocery store down the road. He weighed 7 ¼ pounds. I gutted him and removed his gills. Someone wanted to weigh him again. He still weighed 7 ¼ pounds. We discovered that by turning the fish different ways on the scale, we got different weights. We iced him, and I sent him down to Santa Fe two days later with someone to give to my dad.

Dad got my fish and entered it in a contest at a sporting goods store. The fish weighed in at 7 1/8 pounds at this point. The fish was refrozen in the center of a 300 pound block of ice and put in the window of this sporting goods store. When the ice was about melted, we got the fish and had it mounted. The fish was the largest rainbow trout caught in the state of New Mexico during the month of August. I received a prize of an inscribed Heddon split bamboo rod and reel commemorating this event.

My father was left handed, as was my sister Phyllis. I did some things left handed, some right. I boxed left handed. I batted right. My buddy's folks were giving him golf lessons. He talked me into playing with him, and my dad let me use his left handed clubs. One day we wanted to go play golf, but my dad was out of town and had taken his clubs with him. My buddy's father had brand new right handed clubs; he had given his old set to his son. Still he said, "Go ahead and take my clubs, Bert."

So off I went with my buddy and the clubs. On the second or third hole, I swung and the head of the club went further than the ball did. The shaft was still in my hand. It was a $15.00 club, and I had an allowance of $.50 per week, so all I could see was little dollar signs flying across the sky. I did not play well the rest of that game. His father got the club replaced under warranty, but that episode ended my interest in golf.

I was nearly ten years old in 1929 when the stock market crashed. Most of my teen years were during what is described as the Great Depression. I was fortunate. The highway business was one of the ways the government made work for the poor. My family probably would have been called "well-to-do." We weren't real rich, but we didn't have to skimp. My parents were frugal; the saying at our house was, "It's good to save for a rainy day," meaning to save for hard times. Still, as another saying of those times went, my family could live "high on the hog" to an extent—not throwing money around, but able to do what we liked.

Many families were less fortunate. The Socialist Party slogan in the thirties was they were going to put a "chicken in every pot." Many families were hungry and out of work. From 1934–1936, Oklahoma suffered a major drought. The ground and crops dried up and the sky was filled with red dust. At times it was difficult to breathe. Some days there was so much dust in the air it would be like night in the middle of the day. California started advertising in the Midwest that all kinds of work were available at $5.00 a day if people would just come there. Many families, now called "Okies," picked up what they had left and headed west with signs on their cars "California or bust." When they got to California, the only jobs available were for 5 cents an hour.

9

MY MISSOURI SCHOOLING

There is no frigate like a book
To take us lands away

—Emily Dickinson (1830–1886)

My mother's cousin was Edwin C. Orr, the Prosecuting Attorney at Columbia Missouri. (He always told people that the "C" stood for curiosity.) On a trip through Oklahoma City, he talked my folks into sending my sister Phyllis to the University of Missouri for her last two years of college. My father wanted to break up her current romance with Basil Wilkinson, a man I always admired. While at the University of Missouri, she was homecoming queen. My sister Betty soon followed and was Savitar (Year Book) Queen while she was attending.

I had been given a choice that I could go to Kemper Military School in Boone, Missouri, or to a military school in Roswell, New Mexico. It was my senior year of high school and I really didn't have to take much to graduate, so I did not want to go to either. Betty talked me into going to Kemper as I would be close to her and she would come get me, fix me up with dates, and so on. Basically she got busy and didn't. I went to Kemper Military School at Booneville, Missouri, for one year. I didn't want to go and didn't like it. My room was in a house that had been converted into an overflow dormitory. One of my roommates was a fellow by the name of Boggs from Louisiana, who talked with a slow southern drawl. He was a rounder and quite humorous.

The older cadets were all the time getting him to tell them stories just to hear him talk. Boggs liked to chew tobacco and before long he had half of the school doing it. At this point, the school commandant issued a rule "NO TOBACCO CHEWING." Chewing was not difficult for most of us to give up, but for Boggs it was a different matter. One day we were in the bleachers by the football field studying military science. The instructor, Mr. Fifield, called on Boggs to stand up and answer a question. Boggs was not too sharp, but somebody nearby whispered the answer to him, which he repeated and sat down. Fifield yelled at Boggs, "Stand up, Cadet; I am not through with you. Boggs, are you chewing tobacco?" Boggs clicked his heels and saluted, "No, Sir." The instructor grimaced, "Boggs are you sure you are not chewing tobacco?" Boggs nodded rapidly, "Yes, I am sure I am not chewing tobacco, Sir." Fifield looked down at the ground and kicked the dust with his boots, "Boggs, were you chewing tobacco?" Boggs murmured, "Yes, Sir." Fifield rolled his eyes and kicked the dust again, "How did it taste?" Boggs uttered, "Pretty good, Sir, until I swallowed it when you called on me." Everyone burst into laughter, and Fifield was a good guy and let it go at that.

The room I shared with Boggs and two other fellows was on the first floor with two doors that led into it. We had a wardrobe to hang our clothes in with two drawers in the bottom. Needless to say, we stored any food from home in these drawers. One day we discovered a rat in our room and blocked the cracks under the doors. Then the four of us went after it trying to kill it by hitting it with our shoes. The rat finally jumped up and went out the window. This incident happened during quiet hour when we were supposed to be studying. We attracted a bit of attention, but did not get into trouble.

The side door of our room led into a dark hallway to the latrine. Towards the end of the year, we were issued linseed oil to polish our rifle stocks. We had to find something to store the oil in. The older cadre in the other downstairs room found a dead soldier (empty whiskey bottle) and used that. Among Boggs' other habits, he liked to drink, so these older boys decided to have some fun with him. They caught him in the dark hallway and showed him the bottle. Boggs pleaded with them for a drink. No, they wouldn't let him have it and he kept pleading. They kept it up for some time. Boggs finally pled, "Just let me have a smell." They agreed, starting to put the open whiskey bottle up to his nose. Boggs grabbed their hands and tilted the bottle up and drank half of it before they could stop him. Needless to say, we had one very sick Boggs hanging out our bedroom window all night.

Since my sister Betty was still attending the University of Missouri at Columbia after my senior year at Kemper, I went there too. I joined the Pershing Rifles (a crack ROTC unit), and in our initiation, my roommate and I climbed up the fire escape, ran across the roof of Jesse Hall (a three story administration building), and flew a pair of autographed panties from the flagpole. I will never know why we didn't fall off and break our necks as it was an extremely steep tile roof. I did not go on and try to get my ROTC commission, as without glasses, I was legally blind in both eyes—20-410. I did correct with glasses to 20-20. I always had a big problem with continual headaches. I had been checked for brain tumors and so on, but without a solution. I would wear my glasses just to shoot a rifle, drive a car, or go to the movies.

Betty married Glenn G. Vallentine from Webster Groves, Missouri, on the spur of the moment in February 1940. They were supposed to drive to Springfield Missouri, from Oklahoma City, meet his folks, find a Justice of the Peace, and get married. Phyllis' current boy friend Doug wanted to go, but his boss said he couldn't have Friday off, just the weekend. The wedding party was to leave early Friday morning and get to Springfield in time to make wedding arrangements for Saturday morning. I was to stay and drive with Doug when he got off work. On Friday, the wedding party was slow getting away from Oklahoma City and then they stopped in Tulsa for a long lunch. When they got to Springfield, Glenn's parents had decided no one was coming and had driven back to Webster Groves near St. Louis. So the wedding party went on to St. Louis arriving at Glenn's parents determined to take their vows the next morning.

Doug and I left Friday evening and drove to Springfield, only to find we had to go on to St. Louis. We made the wedding party brunch late Saturday morning. The Justice of the Peace married Glenn and Betty after the brunch and everyone began to celebrate. Doug, who had driven all the way, was really tired by now. Still he insisted we leave that night so he could get back. I got behind the wheel and he curled up in the back. We hadn't gotten far when his car started heating up. I shook him awake. "Drive slow," he muttered, "and wake me when you get to the next gas station." Whenever I got to a gas station, he staggered out and put some water in the radiator. "Drive on," he would command. Soon the car would heat up again. If we asked for a mechanic, we would be told, "Well, there is one fifteen miles back the way you have come or twenty miles ahead." The only variation on this refrain that we would get would be the number of miles back or ahead. With Phil's boyfriend not in good standing with his boss, we just kept trying to head home so he would not miss work Monday. We finally got as far as Lebanon, Missouri, which sat back off the road. We had heard a good mechanic was there. When we got to the main street, it was about two or three a.m., so we pulled out into the middle to look both directions for the garage. About that time, a police car whipped around and pulled in front of us. Two policemen with drawn guns ordered us out of the car and insisted they see the title of the car. After a frantic search, we determined we didn't have it. Right then and there, we should have had them lock us up, so we could eat and sleep, but we didn't. Somehow they were convinced we were having car trouble and needed to get back to

Oklahoma City. Sadly the mechanic there wasn't interested in servicing a car at four a.m., nor on Sunday any time, so we chugged on to Springfield.

We left the car at a radiator place that morning whose proprietor had begrudgingly stated he would have it fixed by afternoon. We checked into a motel to sleep, but got up hopefully about two p.m. and went to the garage. The car wasn't ready until late evening. Once we got started, a pelting snow began and the roads became slushy and hard to maneuver. At Tulsa, the carburetor started acting up and we were forced to stop at another garage. The mechanic there fixed the carburetor, smiled at our pathetic offering of all remaining funds, took half of them and a Canadian quarter, and sent us on our way. Just outside of Oklahoma City, we gassed up and blew the last of the money that we had on something to eat, so we would be truly broke. In our despair, this act seemed grandly fitting. The rest of the wedding party had left late Sunday morning, passed us unknowingly, and now welcomed us back.

My wife of 60 years, Mary Roberta Kyger

We were married at Mary Bob's parents, Dr. and Mrs. Fred Burke Kyger's home in Kansas City, Missouri, 637 West 67 th Street Terrace, on December 28, 1940.

10

WORLD WAR II

Why should the strong—
The beautiful strong—
Why should they not have the flowers?"

—Stephen Crane (1971–1900)

I had an office job at Allied Materials in Oklahoma City, after Mary Bob and I were married.

"Bert, you should enlist right now," said T.A. Nicolson, my constant adviser at Allied and a Commander in the Naval Reserve. "If you don't enlist now, you will be drafted. You will be a lot better off with your background to enlist now than to wait."

On December 14, 1941, only 7 days after Pearl Harbour I enlisted. As a private, I received $21 a month until I finished basic training and then received a raise of $7, for the grand total of $28 a month. Because I was married, I received $15 a month marriage allowance if my wife was with me. I could also get a $30 rent allowance to live off base.

I believe one can't live through a war or even basic training without becoming fatalistic. I was sent to Camp Roberts, California. My bunk mate, Liebst, had been a cook on the Santa Fe El Capitan Train. He had no living relatives, and the closest person to him was a prostitute in Los Angeles. He was desperate to see combat, but never did. After basic, he was assigned to troops guarding the California Coast against attack. Not happy, he volunteered for the paratroopers and was sent to Fort Benning, Georgia. Just when he was supposed to make his first jump, he caught a cold and couldn't go. He was marked, "Barracks" for a week. His fellow paratroopers kept coming back with broken arms and legs until Liebst lost his nerve. He was sent back to guard the California coast. Liebst did finally get to Australia and island hopped his way across the Pacific, but it was always after the fighting was over. Liebst's "poor" luck would not be mine.

My fatalism increased one day my platoon was practicing rapid firing rifles with dummy ammunition. The targets were above ground with a screen that could be raised or lowered. Usually, the target operators stood behind the screens. One of the Corporals decided to sit down, rather than stand, when he raised his screen. A shot rang out scoring a perfect bullseye on his target with live ammunition. That incident shut down practice and scared a lot of us. "Where did that one live round come from?" Often in the service, I found that there weren't always answers, just fortune. Maybe it was this attitude that helped me to survive.

Another time we had the trainees out throwing offensive grenades that were nothing more than a quarter pound block of TNT with a triggering device that had about a three second fuse. After the trainees got through, we had a bunch of "grenades" left that we didn't want to cart back, so the cadre got up there with about three of us in a one man position. Some one would yell and we would all throw at once. Things were fine until the guy to my left instead of throwing overhand as he was supposed to do came around sidearm and let go about four inches in back of my head. The TNT hit me, banged off my helmet liner (we didn't have our steel helmets on), and gave me a nice goose egg. In addition, none of us knew where this block of TNT had gone, so we just went down (it could have been dropping on top of us), but luckily it bounced and went off out in front of us.

My wife, Mary Bob, caught pneumonia right after I went into the service, so she went home to her parents to recover. As soon as she got well, she came out to see me. My platoon Sergeant was about five feet tall with what some call a "short man's" attitude. He was always good to me and nothing would do, but that Mary Bob would stay with his wife in their mobile home. These accommodations gave me quite an inside track.

I still remember when Mary Bob was to leave I caught the flu. The Sergeant, his wife, and Mary Bob, were worried about me, so they gave me an old farmer's cure—a half pint of whiskey and about twice that of hot lemon juice. I had to drink it all. I sweated that flu right out that night. The bedcovers had to be wrung out. But I was cured!! Or at least was not up to another treatment and thought I was cured.

Before Mary Bob came back, I wanted to find a place to rent outside of Camp Roberts. Housing there was at a premium, so I had to help this guy dig sewer and water lines to have the privilege of renting a two room cabin from him. The bedroom held a double bed shoved up against the wall to allow Mary Bob and I space to get in and out of bed. The other room served as living room, dining room and kitchen. We had an ice box that we had to buy a block of ice to cool.

So divine was this cabin that Mary Bob's mother, Lucile Kyger, visited us and claimed that we could grab a cat by its tail, swing it around our heads, and no matter where we let it go, it would find a crack to get out. She was not too pleased with her daughter's accommodations or with my enlistment.

When my basic training was over, I asked to be sent to Fort Benning, Georgia. I got two sets of orders. One set sent me to the 87th Mountain Infantry (ski troopers) who were ready at Seattle, Washington to embark. To this day, I have never been on a pair of skis. This unit never saw combat, but guarded the Aleutian Islands. My other orders were to Fort Benning, supposedly a one way ticket to the front lines.

In the interim, I was in a holding company. Many of the people in it were being put out under Section 8. To avoid their company, I tried to eat most of my meals at my old mess hall or at the NCO Club from then on. When I got to Benning, the medical staff refused to assign me because of my eyes, so I was sent back to California as a NCO instructor. The group I was to instruct was supposedly a "headquarter" company made up of the top 10% of recruits. Getting into it was hard. If it was already full, recruits could be smarter than anyone in that company, but still get assigned to another rifle company. Timing determined a lot of placements. The platoon sergeant at Roberts was regular army. He had been a boxer and was considered "punchy." He would be given special assignments so that I could be put in charge of the platoon.

One day we were teaching the trainees how an unarmed man could disarm another soldier with a bayonet rifle. We did the disarmament demonstration in slow motion with the scabbard over the bayonet. One trainee insisted this one system wouldn't work. The Captain picked me and one of the judo instructors to demonstrate it again. The trainee still commented, "That won't work. Do it faster and see. Besides you have the scabbard on, so it covers up what will really happen." The Captain was mad, "Bert, take that scabbard off and have Jake really come after you. Jake, lunge at Bert." The judo instructor lunged, and I managed to fend the bayonet off, but instead of tripping over my hip and leg like he was supposed to do, Jake crashed into me. We found ourselves in a wrestling match for the rifle. The rifle sight ripped my throat and I had to go to FirstAid. The trainee had convinced me that I could have been speared like a marshmallow using that technique.

The draft, once begun, was supposed to cover people from 18 to 35 years old, single at first, then married, then married with children. However when certain draft boards ran out of people that fit these categories, they took those available. We had quite a few people who had been drafted that were in their mid-forties.

Six that were drafted were 48 years old. One man who had enlisted was 54. Another enlistee was 35 years old with a bad heart. We would go out and march about two blocks and he would keel over. Then we would have to get him to the medics. They would keep him for a couple of days and send him back.

I was assigned to a troop train while I was at Camp Roberts to take some soldiers who had just completed their basic training to Jackson, Mississippi. The train first went north to Oregon, then south to Salt Lake, then north again, then south again. It chugged just about everywhere but Kansas City where Mary Bob was visiting. When the train finally got to Jackson two weeks later, after spending much time parked on various sidings waiting for other trains to pass, the troops were dropped off. I took that train into New Orleans and caught a train there, which arrived back at Camp Roberts in about three days.

While we were still at Camp Roberts, Mary Bob wanted to have a baby. Instead she miscarried. As soon as she could, she wanted to try again, and some time after she got pregnant. Then we were transferred to Camp Blanding, Florida. We drove. Gas rationing was in effect and we were given just enough coupons to get us there. We soon found we had a problem. The coupons were for seventeen gallons and we had a twenty gallon tank. If our tank wasn't really close to empty, we still had to give up our coupon along with the gallons needed to get to Florida. We certainly learned to watch the empty/full status of our tank.

We were allowed some extra time to get to Blanding, so we decided that we would drive through Bakersfield and then come back north and go through Yosemite National Park, some places we wanted to see. Just before we got to Yosemite, we stopped at a bed and breakfast place to spend the night. They informed us that Yosemite was closed. We would either have to travel a long way back, or we could go on a backcountry road near the park that would wind around over to Highway 50. We chose this route and started early the next morning, traversing a mostly one lane road with many hair pin curves whose barren landscape inhabitants were multiple wildcats. We were glad to get to Reno, Nevada, close to midnight. I am convinced that we spent the night there in a whorehouse as doors banged and voices laughed in and out of this seedy hotel all night long. When we got to Salt Lake City, we discovered that one of our tires was bald and another one not much better. Tires were rationed too. Fortunately we were finally able to buy two used tires and continue on.

When we got to Kansas City, some friends of the Kygers, Mary Bob's parents, were in the tire recapping business and got four good tires for us "under the table." We made it the rest of the way to Florida without problems.

We found a place to stay in Gainesville, Florida. The heater was a coal stove, which was hard to keep going. My biggest problem was that I had to be on the post by six a.m.. The post was across 35 miles of open range, which was often foggy in the morning, sometimes limiting visibility to the hood ornament of the car. From Camp Blanding, I was sent to Camp Robinson, Arkansas. Since Mary Bob was nearing her due date, she went directly home to Kansas City from Florida.

Mary Bob and Bert Brooks Jr. on base

11

MY FIRST CHILD

"Bert, Bert Brooks, your family called. Your wife is in labor." That was the message on July 17, 1944, but my status was that as long as I was on bivouac that was where I would stay. About 7 p.m. I was on my way from Camp Robinson, Arkansas, to Research Hospital in Kansas City to see my wife and new daughter Barbara Lucile. The night was almost cloudless, starlit with just a sliver of a moon. About 2 a.m., I was nearly to Branson, Missouri, roaring down a steep hill to cross a little bridge. Whoa, did I wake up! Black shapes filled the whole left side of the road. I slammed on the brakes and swerved to the left. More black figures were approaching the left shoulder. I laid on my horn. I was not slowing down fast enough. Several of the little Angus steers on the left began to move off, but one large cow just stood and stared reprovingly at the careening evening indignity shattering her quiet. Somehow I slid between her and the tiny calves on the right shoulder. I could not believe my luck. Chastened, I continued on my way to see my own dear family.

About the first of September Mary Bob brought Barbara Lu to Little Rock, which was a happy reunion. Mary Bob did not like the place in town that I had been able to find and refused to stay in it. So we found a motel way out the other side of town toward Hot Springs. The lady who ran it had had some drunks there the night before and was disgusted, so she rented a room to us on a permanent basis.

While at Camp Robinson, I had the dubious distinction of being sent to a school on venereal disease. If nothing else, it made a believer out of me. At any rate, at the end of the day before being dismissed, the troops would line up on the company street. I got out in front of them and lectured them on the safeties of sex. Their wives and girlfriends stood right behind me, waiting for me to get through and hearing all I had to say. My lecture had not been designed as a uni-sex lecture. I blushed to my boots every time I gave this talk. The army's position which I had to yell out was, "You cannot get venereal disease without having sex!

Understand that, Soldier! You have to have SEX to get venereal disease." Right away a trainee proved me wrong by catching gonorrhea in his eyes and no place else. After my talks, chigger bites often appeared to be syphilis chancres and were reported to the amused medics.

Bert Brooks, Jr. holds Barbara Lu at three months old, just before he embarks for the front lines.

Bert Brooks, Jr. holds Barbara Lu while home from bivouac July 24, 1944 in her grandparents, Fred and Lucile Kyger's backyard

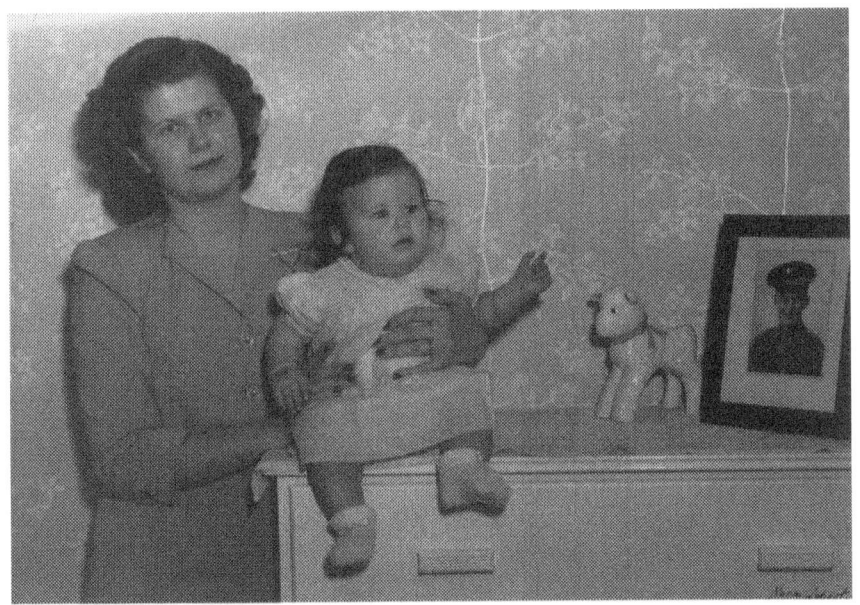

Mary Bob Brooks and Barbara Lu await Bert Brooks, Jr.'s return from overseas.

12

OVERSEAS

No mockeries now for them; no prayers nor bells,
Nor any voice of mourning save the choirs—
The shrill, demented choirs of wailing shells;

—Wilfred Owen (1893–1918)

In November of 1944, nearly three years after I had joined, I was ordered to the port of embarkation. I took Mary Bob and Barbara Lu to Oklahoma City and saw my mother and then went to a town in New Jersey and from there to Boston, Massachusetts. I was acting First Sergeant of a company that had two real characters in it. One was being treated for syphilis. One day he had just gotten tired and walked off guard duty. The officers decided not to court martial him, but to put him on constant KP on ship, expecting him to get killed in combat anyhow. Another called "Mikey the Mouth" was on KP with him. Both decided they were going to shoot me in the back the first chance they had when we got to the front, "Hey, Sergeant," they would croon, "better watch your back." Luckily the latter soldier got shipped somewhere else, and the one with syphilis found he had it in the bones of his feet and was hospitalized.

We went over on the second fastest cruise ship that England had and did not go in a convoy as this ship could outrun a submarine. We landed in Scotland and traveled across it and England by train arriving in a camp in Liverpool about 2:00 a.m. in the middle of the winter. We were assigned to tents that had little charcoal stoves in them. Nobody could start the charcoal. Finally someone found a garden hose and we cut it in pieces and the charcoal began to smolder. At approximately the same time that we got our fires started, we heard the call for breakfast. We ate and got on shipboard again. Chilling cold was our constant companion from that night on.

From Liverpool, we went to Le Havre, France. We were told that the citizens there didn't like Americans very much. The Germans had pulled out of Le Havre without American knowledge and we had bombed the entire area. After spending a night in Le Havre, we were loaded in boxcars and probably went through the outskirts of Paris. We stole some potatoes out of another train and built a fire right on the floor of the boxcar. The Battle of the Bulge had begun. We arrived at a replacement camp where we received physical exams. The eye doctor swore, "Whoever sent you here was totally crazy. You should never be on the front lines, boy," but the next day I was on my way.

I was assigned to the Third Infantry division, which was both the most decorated division in the war and had the highest number of casualties. Starting with Africa, the Third made all of the landings in the European theater, with the exception of Normandy. The Third Division was part of Patch's Seventh Army, which was attached to the Free French. The Third was now a part of the Battle of the Bulge. We were at the end of the line, next to Switzerland, in Alsace-Lorraine, and in what was called the Colmar pocket. Switzerland was on our right flank and Patton in France on our left and the Rhine River separated us from Germany.

A temporary company was formed to keep us until the division pulled back in the next day or two. I was First Sergeant of it. The commanding officer was a First Lieutenant Hammond, who had landed in Africa, in Salerno, in Anzio, and in Southern France. He had been at all the big fights with the exception of Normandy and was a regimental officer. For the short time we knew each other, we became good friends.

Lieutenant Hammond told me about the Moroccans that were with the Free French, "If they pull out their knife to show it to you, they have to draw blood before putting it away. Often they just nick their fingers. When I was with the French, they would be sent out on night missions. They would find two or three Germans sleeping in a foxhole and cut all but one's throat, leaving him to awake surrounded by the dead." Hammond went on, "These Moroccans were very unnerving. They could trot alongside their donkeys all day long through the mountains. And they liked to smoke. We often saw their cigarettes glow in the dark."

Speaking of smoking, I would say that 95% of us in the services smoked. I get angry sometimes that smokers are held in such disrepute today when these are the people who fought for our liberty. And I think the fuss about second hand smoke is ridiculous. I did quit smoking a year ago. I always knew that smoking was not good for me. I made the choice to smoke and later made the choice to quit. I don't believe half of what is said about smoking and feel the government should not mandate personal choices.

The day after our physicals we were kept standing out in this bitter cold for over two hours to be welcomed by the Division General. When he got there, he informed us, "You are probably not going to live. Your odds in the battles to come are very slim. You should give your parents the consolation that you fought like men. My son was a paratrooper who was killed jumping into Belgium. My wife and I console ourselves with his courage and bravery. Give your parents that consolation."

When I went up to the front, I was allowed my weapon of choice and chose a Thompson submachine gun, 45 caliber. I had always been taught that the First Sergeant, the Supply Sergeant, and the Company Clerk stayed behind the lines (which did not turn out to be the truth for me), and a Tommy gun had seemed more suitable for that location. I had had very little training with a Tommy gun at Fort Benning, but felt that it was the weapon for close infighting in the night. However, it could go through an awful lot of ammunition in a hurry. I soon found that by holding low to the left side of my target the gun would pull up to the right and would space my shots four-six inches apart. I would generally fire it in bursts of three to six bullets.

The next day I was assigned to a company that needed a First Sergeant. The First Sergeant stayed up with the troops and the Company Clerk stayed behind the lines. I never saw him. We had been built up to a full company strength of 173 to 176 men. The first night we were as far in reserve as we could get and were told to take up positions and dig slit trenches. Most of us had a little tiny pack shovel. In the glacial temperature, the ground was frozen down two or three feet. After an hour, all of us had a bare six inch outline of a slit trench. Most of the guys gave up and just laid down. About that time, we were given our first German presence when they opened fire at us with antiaircraft guns or artillery that was hitting the trees and giving aerial bursts.

Our routine was that, in every other fox hole, one man would sleep in the fox hole and the other would stand guard outside. I was to have one of the guards wake me every hour, tell me the password, and then I would go around and check the other guards. I would come back and crawl into my sleeping bag and fall asleep for a few minutes. Soon I would be shaken to go check again. One night there was an aerial burst that went off close to two of my men, and the one that was out murmured, "Boy, that was close—are you all right?" His buddy answered, "Yeah," but in reality he had been hit in the temple by a piece of shrapnel. He laid there and bled to death while his bunkmate stayed on watch.

After that incident, my bunkmate and I got a full size shovel and an axe. Our slit trenches were two and one half feet deep, and we chopped trees and put a roof on them with dirt and snow on top. When we slept, we slept with our feet by the opening. The ground was frozen all the way down, and we would take the plastic mustard gas sheets, lay them on the ground, and put our sleeping bags on top of them. Otherwise, the heat from our bodies would melt the moisture in the ground and soon we would be sleeping in puddles of water. We climbed fully dressed, boots and all, into our sleeping bags. We only took off our overcoats, which we placed on top of the sleeping bags, covering the openings for our faces. We took our rifles, or as in my case, Tommy guns into the sleeping bags. We would be sleeping with grenades, pistols, and knives, whatever we had.

My bunkmate was a telephone lineman stringing wire, which he left to do early each morning and then I would see him at night to help me to dig in. As soon as we were dug in, we tried to sleep. On awakening, he would be off, so I scarcely saw him. In that cold, the two of us seldom could sleep for forty-five minutes without having to get out and relieve ourselves. We were completely exhausted. Our rations left much to be desired. As a consequence, we did not eat a lot of solid food and could go a long time without exposing our bare rears to the freezing cold. Sometimes, after we took a town, we would "liberate" chickens, eggs, or other food. We never saw any civilians in these towns. Despite news accounts to the contrary in the *Stars and Stripes* and other U.S. newspapers, we often lacked warm clothing. We took winter combat jackets off the dead, and the wounded left theirs for the men that were still fighting.

One night we had taken up temporary positions and were starting a slit trench when the Germans started laying down some mortar fire. My lineman "bunkie" and I climbed into the little hole we had achieved, and some poor guy from the engineers piled in on top of us. He had to be mostly above ground. A mortar shell landed twelve inches from our slit trench, but it was a dud. That day fate intervened on one soldier's side.

The Third Division had no armor, but we did have some tank destroyers, which were very similar, except they are not nearly as heavily armored. In general, we attacked at night while I was there and slept during the day. The Third Division took Salzburg, Austria, and turned it over to other American troops who were promptly kicked out by the Germans. We had to go back and take it again. Some divisions only attacked in the daytime (which is hard for me to imagine and seems pretty stupid).

One day we were out in the edge of a woods when two or three German Tiger tanks pulled out in front of us. We had been exchanging shots with them. Suddenly they pulled back, headed off toward our left flank, and disappeared. We kept watching for them to show up again, when suddenly this whole armored column showed up on our left flank. We fought for two hours before we found out they were the Free French. They didn't do any damage to us, but we sure did to them. And we got a good lesson in what armor piercing shells sound like whistling off through the woods.

One day we attacked this little French village close to Colmar. Whoever was there had not put up much resistance, and suddenly all shooting had stopped. When we got to this house on the edge of town, we just milled around it, wondering where the Germans had gone. Finally one of us went over by the door to the cellar of this house and yelled "Kommen sie aus mit das hand hoch" and about fifty German soldiers came out with their hands up as asked. They had been sitting in a wine cellar, getting drunk, waiting for us to come and get them.

The Allies were not allowed to bomb or shell Colmar as there were a couple of big American plants there. One of them might have been General Motors. We, the Americans, were not allowed to enter Colmar, but had to completely surround it, with the Germans fleeing out just before we closed the trap. The Free French went in and celebrated for three or four days, while we went on without them.

Every week to ten days, we would get replacements to build us to full company strength, somewhere around 176 men. The first day in combat (which was always the next day) we would never have more than 76–77 men left. Our company would continue fighting, often dwindling down to as low as fifteen men, but usually closer to 25 to 35 of us, still doing the same job originally given to 176 men. On the first day, many of those lost were injured, not dead. After that, the dead seemed to increase rapidly. I felt this statistic was because the enemy just sprayed the area in the beginning, without particularly aiming. As we became fewer, each individual became a defined target. I learned quickly that those firing usually sought out the largest group and often overlooked a lone man. I started keeping to myself.

13

THE SILVER STAR

Yes; quaint and curious war is!
You shoot a fellow down
You'd treat, if met where any bar is,
Or help to half-a-crown.

—Thomas Hardy (1840–1928)

Another night we were attacking a different village. The Germans had brought in crack ski troops to throw against us. As we approached this village in the early morning hours, a German tank opened fire on us. I hit the ground and a shell landed in front of me about five feet away. It exploded and the blast went out and over me. The powder from the explosion burnt my face and blackened my glasses, as well as the sight and other parts of my Tommy gun.

Some troops were starting to work their way into town over on my right, and I went with them. I later found out they were a different company. When we got on the main street, there were houses and cover on one side but none on the other. So I went out in the open. A German machine gun nest was in a house down the street. I opened fire on it and continued to advance, but the other troops across the street with the cover wouldn't come. As it turned out, their reticence was for the best. The Germans were interested in shooting at the bunch rather than the one guy out in the open by himself.

Two Germans came out into the middle of the street with a white flag, but also carrying a light machine gun. Eventually they dropped down and started shooting at us. They were quite visible to me though, so they retreated. I was about out of ammunition by this time, but felt that I had them on the run. I had a "liberated" pistol that was loaded and hand grenades, so I kept going. I put a couple of grenades in the house and then went around to the courtyard where I found two of them that I had wounded. One was shot through the lower abdomen, and as I tried to help him he died. The other was shot sideways through both eyes and the bridge of his nose. A 45 caliber bullet makes a hell of a hole. I didn't have the slightest idea how I could patch him up and wound up doing nothing. It sounded horrible, listening to him try to breathe. Later I sent a medic to him.

I went back out to the street and saw some troops finally starting to come up. They were my company and just now coming into town. They set up company headquarters where I had wiped out the machine gun nest. That day First Lieutenant Hammond who was attached to the regiment that had made all of the landings came down, and the officers told him about my taking the machine gun nest. I wound up with a Silver Star.

14

THE SPRING THAW

Some say the world will end in fire,
Some say in ice.

—Robert Frost (1874–1963)

I have failed to mention that through the time I was in combat, I never had a Company Commander who lived more than five days; one was with us only six hours. The Company Commander was the lead officer and the First Sergeant was generally right with him. No one really had any opportunity to know anyone. The Platoon Lieutenant's life span was not much greater than the Company Commander's. Our company had almost a complete turnover every week to ten days from losses. One day, the Captain sent me out to look over a bunch of corpses from our company to see if I could recognize any of them. The chances of identifying one's fellow company men were poor to next to none, as most of them had often just arrived.

One night, when the Captain was in the front of this single file column leading us in an attack, he led us down into this valley and ran into Jerry's final protective line and got shot up. I was in the middle of the company which hadn't even started into the valley. Most of the men were able to back out and milled around out in the open on the top of this hill like a bunch of sheep. They were an excellent target. I tried to stay by myself and moved away from them. Down in the valley, men were yelling for a medic. Finally our company moved off to one side and flanked the Germans, forcing them to move so that the medic could go in for the injured.

When the spring thaw came, we sank into the mud up to our knees. As we lifted our boots, the mud would suck and slurp, trying to pull them off. The motion of the boots completely skinned the heels of my frozen feet. In our division, the rule was "No soldier reports to First Aid with frozen feet if he can still walk." Our casualties were so high that the odds we were going to be wounded and could be treated for both the wound and the feet at the same time seemed common sense. Dead men didn't need to worry about frozen feet. This philosophy worked for all but those to whom the great probabilities did not happen. When a man couldn't walk on his frozen stubs, the probability was that his legs would be amputated.

One night we went into attack, and some idiot officer at regiment had the brilliant idea of lining all of these searchlights up behind us. He proclaimed that when the lights were turned on, they would blind the enemy and we could charge forward. Well, I am not to judge if the enemy was even startled, but each of us became a distinct silhouette. Needless to say, that plan went by the wayside. Another plan my company refused to follow was that of the rolling barrage. Supposedly, the artillery would shoot 100 feet in front of us and as we moved up they would lift and shoot another 100 feet further out. We had heard of too many cases where the artillery didn't move up. We did call the Air Force to bomb right out in front of us on occasion.

My last night in combat we had lost our company commander, and at nine p.m., a new First Lieutenant Koch from regiment came down and took over as Company Commander. We moved out from this little town to attack almost immediately. It was after the thaw and tough going. Luckily, I was in the front of the column with Lieutenant Koch which meant the ruts were just being formed and so walking was easier. We were supposed to find a bridge across a river and take it. We got up on this hill above the river, and Lieutenant Koch had me pick a man from the lead platoon to take with me. We were to scout ahead and find the bridge. After we got to the river, we were to work our way to the left. On the river banks, we found ourselves in some low lying marsh ground that was covered with very tall weeds. Try as we might, we couldn't move without making a little bit of noise. The Germans were at the bridge and heard us. They machine gunned our area. Both of us hit the ground. Mud splattered from the bullets up into our whitened faces. I decided we better slip out of there without shooting back, hoping the Germans might think some animal had made the noise. When we got back, we found the company pulling out. We ran into the middle of it. Lieutenant Koch had been walking around checking the positions that the platoons had taken up when the Germans had opened up on us. They had killed him a thousand feet or more behind us. He arrived at 9 p.m. and died at 3 a.m. after having made it all the way from an African landing.

The two Lieutenants that were left, pulled the troops out in the reverse order of the way we had gone in. They hadn't thought of the scouting party. If we had been just a little bit more cautious on that marsh or a little bit slower coming back, we would have found ourselves abandoned. My company was on the tail of the line coming out. I was exhausted from the scouting, so instead of walking down there and walking back, I walked on with the men we had met. The Lieutenant who was leading just kept going.

He finally ran into what was left of F Company (seven men) and picked them up and took us back to the town we had left, telling us to go back to the houses we had bunked in the day before. Then he went to report to battalion headquarters.

The other Lieutenant had stopped the tail end of the column which included my company and had not come back with us. Headquarters told the reporting Lieutenant to pick us all back up, along with F Company, and join the platoon that had stayed behind. He was to try to relieve C Company that had gotten through to its objective. The Lieutenant picked up those companies he knew to be there, but five of us belonged to company headquarters. He didn't realize that he had brought us back.

The next morning we five checked in at battalion headquarters and were told to join our company. However, there was a bridge at the edge of town that we would have to cross and the Jerrys (nickname for the Germans) were laying a barrage down on it. We were told to wait until evening and go up with the Supply Sergeant.

Since I had until evening, I and another guy who wasn't feeling well went to the medic. I wanted some adhesive tape for my heels. The doctors would not just give me the adhesive tape, but insisted on seeing my feet and promptly announced that the war was over for me. I might have argued with them. I don't know, but just then, the news came that the entire battalion of 975 men had been wiped out. The five of us were all that was left.

We were taken by ambulance to the rear and then flown to a temporary hospital in Scotland. We arrived at night and were put in a ward and the lights were turned out. Now nobody in this ward was supposed to be able to walk. All our boots had been taken away from us; my thawed feet were screaming with outrage at their condition.

One of the men with us had had his leg amputated, and it started to bleed. We all yelled for help, but we could not raise anyone. So I and two or three others got up and started hobbling through nearby wards (they were separate buildings) trying to find someone. We finally did. The doctors and nurses were having a little social time. We got them back there to take care of him. He had lost so much blood by that time that he was unable to go on with us when we were moved out to England.

I was moved to another hospital near Sheffield, England. It was still cold a good part of this time and those of us with frozen feet (about all us in my ward) slept with the covers folded back from the bottom of the bed about 12 inches, so that our feet weren't covered. Incidentally, the fellow in the bed next to me had been wounded, but was now well and wanted to go back to the front. But when he came into the hospital, his boots had been cut off. His feet were so big that no boots would fit him, so he was stuck in that bed, a barefooted, bigfooted soldier.

Shortly after May 8, 1945 (Veteran's Day) when the Germans surrendered, the hospital was closed down, so the medical staff could go to the Pacific. All ambulatory patients were marked limited duty and sent to a replacement center. The others were flown home.

At the replacement center, I was given guard duty at one of the outside gates. I had a little guard shack and was responsible to see no one came or went through that gate. Orders on the wall stated, "Civilians should be treated courteously but sent to the main gate." One day, a rain shower blew in quickly, and a young lady came over. "Can you let me in here, so I don't get wet," she asked. "No, I'm sorry, but you will have to go around to the main gate," I told her. While she was there, a city bus came by. She left within a minute.

About fifteen minutes later, this jeep full of MP's came up. "Okay, soldier," they said. "You are coming with us." "What for?" I asked. "Listen, don't get smart; just get in this jeep. You have been reported by the Officer of the Day." "I'm not going anywhere until I receive orders from my commanding officer," I replied. Finally they told me that I had been seen fraternizing with a young woman while I was on guard duty. I retorted, "Listen, that girl was here less than a minute, and if you look at those rules written on the wall, I did just what is stated. Furthermore if you try to arrest me before I am properly relieved, I have a loaded rifle in my hands and I will use it." They agreed to stay there until the officer who had filed the complaint came down.

The officer filing the complaint had been on the bus coming back from town. I showed him the orders on the wall and told him I had refused to leave until properly relieved. He growled, "I will get those orders changed." I wonder if he changed them to shoot the next civilian that came over to ask a question.

I shipped out the next morning and went to the Military Government in Augsburg, Germany as acting Master Sergeant and head of the Message Center. The offices in Augsburg were located in a hotel on the second floor. The hotel faced a street that ended in a flight of steep cement steps to a restaurant where we ate. Most of the men slept in the upper floors of the hotel. About eight of us were assigned to a mansion on the same street as the restaurant. This period resembled civilian life for us. We had 40 hour work weeks and secretaries. Our waitresses were German, but spoke good English. In fact, even little kids in Augsburg spoke English.

While I was with the Military Government, I read a book filled with photographs of human-skin lampshades and purses from women's breasts found in the concentration camp at Dauchau. I also read the Germans had plans to make a giant space magnifying glass to concentrate the sun's rays on military targets to incinerate them. The illustrations were a sordid indication of what the perverted and prejudiced might justify.

We made a point to carry loaded guns with us wherever we went. My feet were bothering me often, so I went to the Aid station and was given a bottle of half grain codeine tablets. "Take one when you need it," I was told, "maybe two if the pain is bad." From time to time, I would pop one of those pills. I couldn't tell if they had an effect. One day a buddy and I were kidding around on the cement stairs on our way to supper, and he accidentally stepped on my big toe. The pain was so bad that I grabbed my knee and not my toe. The pain cut off the nerves to my foot and locked my knee. When we got into the restaurant, I swallowed two codeine tablets as fast as I could. Suddenly I was on a bad codeine drunk. I never took another tablet.

One of the men in our intelligence division spoke eleven languages, with his English being the worst. He had lived in some little country in central Europe and when the Germans came, he had gone to France, Africa, and finally gotten to Detroit, Michigan where he joined the U.S. Army. One day we all went fishing. He had gotten some fishing poles and some 10 in 1 rations (they fed ten men one day). He took us out into the hills to a little stream. A German farm couple agreed to prepare our rations for us while we fished. When we got back, we learned what expresso was. Try as we might, we could not add enough water to make that coffee drinkable, but we sure tried because our hostess was so amiable.

My feet continued to bother me. Vibration in a car was terrible for me to bear, so the Aid Station sent me to a hospital. After a month, I was marked to be flown home. I was flown into Paris, but the plane landed at the wrong airport for my connecting flight that night. All of the patients on the plane with me were taken to a Paris hospital, but then we found our flight cancelled entirely.

I was left stranded in a hospital in Paris with no clue when I would get home. About six of us shared a hospital room. The soldier next to me had been shot through the eye and had a glass eye. The bullet was still in his head. The staff was afraid to take it out. One of the soldiers was black. I grew up when Green River laws existed and Ku Klux Klan burnings still were known. This brave man was somewhat uncomfortable being with all us whites, perhaps with justification, though we all tried to be friendly.

Some of the men in this hospital frightened me. They told about capturing Germans to take back to the POW camp and shooting them as soon as they and the POWs were out of sight of the main camp. They would laugh, "We just said those murdering Nazis had tried to escape." Others bragged of raping some of the German farm women.

Finally, some of us started to be released on points and sent home. I approached my doctor and asked him if I could go home on points and then check into a hospital after I got to the States. He wouldn't hear of it. Finally in November, all of the patients were assigned to be shipped out. I was to go home on a Hospital Ship. The day before I was to depart, I went to exchange my French currency for American money. When I was there, the officer in charge could not find my name on the list. In fact he couldn't find any record for me. I asked my doctor, and he began asking. Some technician spoke up, "Well, I thought Bert was going home on points. I heard him ask you, so I just tore up his records."

So I couldn't board the ship. I was sent to Antwerp, Belgium, to go home on points. I still remember the waffle with ice cream I ate there while waiting. It was so delicious. At the Port of Embarkation Depot, we were told to turn in any "liberated" guns. These guns would be returned to us stateside. We were told we would be searched as we boarded. I had been told this the first time I had been hospitalized and never saw my guns again, so this time I hid mine. I wasn't searched.

I came back on a Liberty Ship in the middle of the winter on the Atlantic. Bunks were about six high and a man just about had to turn sideways to get down the aisles. We were fed once a day. Split Pea Soup was the usual meal, which met with this refrain: "What'd you have for breakfast?" "Pea Green Soup." "What'd you have for lunch?" "Pea Green Soup" What'd you have for dinner? "Pea Green Soup." What'd you do all night?" We may have made fun of our meal, but it was thick, warm, and good. I don't get sea sick, but most of the men on that ship did. Thus, I spent most of my time on deck in the fresh air. We came in through the port of Boston, and I found out that I was being sent to Camp Chaffee, Arkansas, which is outside of Fort Smith. I called Mary Bob and let her know, but having had previous experience with troop trains, I didn't have the slightest idea when I would get there. My train arrived at night and we were assigned to some barracks. Just as I was getting ready to sack out, some officer came looking for me. He had a pass for me, and Mary Bob was there. Now that was a nice welcome home.

I didn't sign up for the reserve nor did I check into the hospital. I wanted out. I did put in for a partial pension on my feet because I had no idea what future problems I might have, especially with my records torn up. I had gone in on December 14, 1941 and was mustered out on December 14, 1945.

After the war, Mary Bob's father, Dr. Kyger (Daddy Doc to the grandchildren) made a trip to Europe and met some friends he had known in Prague when he was a student there. The women told him that when the Russians captured Prague, all of them were forced down into the basement of their apartment building. The men stood on one side and the women on the other. They held machine guns on them and told them to take off all their clothes. Then the women were taken out one after another and gang raped for three days. Then the men were loaded in box cars and shipped to slave labor camps in Siberia. Most were never heard from again.

I have always felt that God was in everything in the great outdoors. Living through combat makes a person seek God. I felt that God looked out for me and saw me through that horror when there was really no reason for anyone to survive.

January 26, 1947

Barbara Lu outside the Prairie Village house at 4006 West 69th Street that we bought after I got my job at the Marley Company.

15

POST WAR LIFE

Now, of my threescore years and ten,
Twenty will not come again,
And take from seventy springs a score,
It only leaves me fifty more.

—A.E. Housman (1859–1936)

After the war, I started going to night school in Kansas City under the GI Bill taking a full course of 17–18 hours. One of the teachers recommended me for a job. I didn't take it, but decided to start looking. The Marley Company was forming a new department and hired me on April 29, 1946.

I needed a car then since we had sold mine when I left. Cars were hard to get in this postwar period. The Kygers, Mary Bob's parents, were good friends with the Greenleases, owners of a large car dealership in Kansas City, and Mary Bob's brother-in-law George worked for a dealership. Still we couldn't get a car. Finally Harry Rice, a Buick dealer told us that he had a brand new Plymouth sedan that some one in Central Kansas had traded on a Buick and that he would let us have it for what he was allowing on it. He certainly earned our loyalty to Buick.

Soon we bought a house at 4006 West 69th Street in Prairie Village. The cost of houses had doubled during the war. Many of us groused about the financial advantages those who hadn't gone to war had had. The soldiers coming home and setting up house had caused prices to increase rapidly in all areas. The house we bought had sold new for $6,500.00 in 1941 with an electric stove and refrigerator included. In May 1946, Mary Bob and I paid $12,500 for it without the stove and refrigerator. Probably a year earlier, it would have sold at the 1941 price.

My daughter Phyllis was born November 8, 1948, sharing her birth date with Dr. Fred Burke Kyger, Mary Bob's father. I named her Phyllis Katherin Brooks after my sister. I didn't favor this sister over Jane and Betty. I just liked the name.

One Easter, while we were living in Prairie Village, Barbara Lu insisted on leaving a carrot out for the Easter Bunny. Brindle, the Scotty dog I had given Mary Bob, found the carrot and ate about half of it, leaving very definite teeth marks on the remainder and carrot pieces throughout the living room. Barbara squealed, "The Easter Bunny was here!" She was delighted. Even Mary Bob and I wondered a bit if the Bunny had come—what an odd appetite for a Scotty!

My father died in Dallas, Texas, on January 22, 1950, after disowning me and two of my sisters, Phyllis and Jane, in the early 1940's. He hadn't approved of my marriage, saying, "You don't need to buy a cow to get the cream, Bert." When my sister Betty called me, she told me of his death and asked me to meet her in Dallas where he would be cremated. He had never seen my children or me since the time I was disowned. I had to borrow money from my boss Mr. Mart to go, because it was Sunday and the banks were closed. I drove into his house, and he cashed a check for me. I was really surprised to find him and his wife on the same plane with me that afternoon to Dallas. They were taking a short vacation. Neither of us had thought to say where we were going.

Betty and I stayed in a small hotel not too far from the funeral home. My father had remarried, but was in the process of another divorce. My dad's business associates, including Slim Dahlgren, were at the funeral. They took Betty and me back and introduced us to the second Mrs. Brooks. Following the funeral, Dad was cremated. I had read that many bodies were showing up in medical schools that had supposedly been cremated. Thus, I and my cousin Wayne Brooks went to the crematorium and witnessed the cremation. We helped to collect the ashes and returned to the hotel.

That night I couldn't sleep. I kept hearing the fan from the incinerator at the crematorium. I finally gave up and took a walk. Almost immediately, I discovered that my room was right above the exhaust fan of a restaurant. I really was hearing a fan. After that, I got some sleep.

The next day, Betty and I took the ashes that I had kept in my room that night. We hired a plane to fly us over Lake Texhoma to disperse the ashes according to my father's wishes. Slim had planned on going with us, but had to cancel at the last minute, as he had had a mild heart problem. I opened the door of the plane and held the box out. The wind hungrily sucked the ashes. I would not return to this lake until Mary Bob, I, and all of our children and their families celebrated our 60th wedding anniversary there in the summer of 2000.

Despite having disowned three of his four children, Dad did leave all of us some money and Allied stock in his will. Betty got 40% of the total left to his children, because she had always maintained a relationship with Dad, but Jane, Phyllis, and I got 20% each. I always swore I would treat each of my children equally, no matter. Thank goodness, they did not test me. Later I would become a member of the Board of Directors of Allied, a closely held corporation, which paid little or no dividends and, at the start, no directors' fees. The meetings were held in Oklahoma City. My expenses to attend were paid. Later on Allied started paying $100 a meeting extra. I enjoyed these chances to see my mother who still lived in the family home in Oklahoma City.

In 1951, I joined the Masons. My father had belonged to the Masons, the Scottish Rite, and the Shriners. In time I became all three and would be happy if my descendents were members. The Masons' slogan by Ray Denslow is meaningful to me, "I was born in antiquity, in the ancient days when men first dreamed of God. I have been tried through the ages and found true. The crossroads of the world bear the imprint of my feet and the cathedrals of all nations, the skill of my hands." For me, man's progress is marked by each individual's contributions.

I started to look for a place at Lake Lotawana, a lake outside of Kansas City, shortly after Phyllis was born. I found a suitable summer home, and Dr. Kyger bought it and put it in Mary Bob's and her sister June's names. We used to go out there and fish or swim nearly every weekend for the next few years. My son Kyger, now called BK, was born June 14, 1953, on his grandmother, Lucile Kyger's birthday. My nephew Fred, June and George's eldest, called the Lotawana house, the "Lotawork" house, because he had to cut the steep lawn down to the dock.

Dr. Kyger had bought a fishing boat that I wanted for the place. Two or three years later, my brother-in-law George talked Dr. Kyger into trading "my" boat in on a bigger one that could not be used for fishing. I bought my own, and a year or so later we moved to the farm and quit going to the lake.

Fred Green (June Kyger and George Green's oldest boy) and Barbara Lu at Lake Lotawana near Kansas City

The family gathered to celebrate Bert and Mary Bob Brooks' 60th wedding anniversary 1940–2000 at Lake Texhoma in the summer of 2000. From left are Ashley Meredith Little and her mother Phyllis Katherin Brooks Little. Kloe Marie Brooks is sitting on Phyllis' son Kyle's shoulders and Kyle's arm is on Daniel Boone Brooks; these are Bert Kyger (B.K.) and Elizabeth (Beth) Sylvester Brooks' children. Mary Bob and Bert are sitting. Elisebeth Ayn (Beth) Nielsen stands behind them with her parents John David (Jack) and Barbara Nielsen. Sara Nielsen and Chris Nielsen Collins are on each side of B.K. Michael Collins holds his son, the first great grandchild, Cameron John Collins, born 3-22-2000.

16

TORNADO

Apparently with no surprise
To any happy flower,
The frost beheads it at its play
In accidental power.

—Emily Dickinson (1830–1886)

In 1951, I bought 80 acres outside of Stanley, Kansas, at what is now 175th Street and Switzer (originally Terry Road). Only an old barn was on the place. We would not build and move there until 1956 at the end of Barbara's sixth grade year, but we began spending our weekends there. I bought a paint horse called Butterball and a Shetland pony. The pony rolled over every time it was saddled, wreaking havoc on the saddle, frightening potential cowgirls, and winning immediate resale.

We moved in the summer of 1956 to what would be our family home until my son was in his freshman year of high school and my two daughters were married. Then Mary Bob, Kyger (B.K.), and I would move to Stockton, California, upon my promotion to Vice-President at the Marley Complany plant there.

In the spring of 1957, Barbara, her friend Merry Uphaus, and Phyllis were putting the horses away. Barb slapped Ginger on her haunches after currying her, "Good night, girl, run on off to the pasture with your colt." Phil slipped off her seventeen hand high mount Black Beauty that she often rode bareback and crawled right under her. "It sure seems calm out," she murmured. Merry had ridden the paint Butterball. All three girls started up to the house.

When they entered, I was watching the news on television; we had gotten a 12" screen console in 1948, which was blurting a tornado warning, "A tornado has been sighted on the ground southwest of Stillwell, Kansas." Stillwell was to the south of us. "Mary Bob," I yelled, "maybe you better get Kyger out of the tub. I am going to go outside and take a look." The girls trailed along behind me. The day was windless with blue sky overhead, but dark, black clouds rolled off to the west over the hedge tree row. "Get downstairs, girls," I yelled. "Hurry up, Mary Bob; just get a towel around Kyg and get downstairs." She came running down, trying to bundle our nearly four year old son in her arms. I went back for one more glance and then ran to the basement where everyone was huddled in the southwest corner as advised. My heart was beating quickly, for I had nearly run upstairs mistakenly.

Just then a hissing wind seemed to snake down on the house, beating sticks and icy hail balls against the windows. Then came utter quiet. We all went out and stood on the lawn and watched a huge funnel cloud move slowly towards Kansas City. Large ice chunks lay on the ground and an eerie red sun lit up a destructive trail. I walked up the driveway to get the paper and to get my bearings. Our neighbor's detached garage had an enormous tree deposited right on top of it. I looked down the road and aluminum roofing strips were wrapped around the telephone poles. Merry Uphaus' parents drove up, "Is everyone all right?" They had come to get Merry and hold her tight.

I realized I had no idea where the horses were. I got a flashlight and headed down towards the bottom pasture. The old barn was totally gone, hardly a hay straw to mark its existence. The fences lay in disarray. Finally in my neighbor's pasture, I found the two colts, Dee Day and Sunny Star, their little bodies broken and mangled. The vet came from Martin City, but his only advice was "We'll have to put them down," which he did.

The man who farmed our ground Aime Verhaeghe came down. It was dark now. He and his family had been in their storm cellar. Winding across the pasture in the vet's pickup, the three of us started looking for the other horses, trying to follow the tornado's path. Barbara's horse Ginger suddenly came into our headlights, standing with her head down and her feet spread. She had a 2" x 6" just behind her left shoulder, going forward at an angle. The vet Bill Stewart pulled it out and cleaned out the gaping wound, "I don't think it punctured her body cavity, Bert. You should try to clean her out every day. She may live." It was after midnight and we gave up our search for the other horses. "I'll be back in the morning," he said. "Thanks, Bill," I stuttered. As he drove off, I realized I was alone in the dark on an extremely rough piece of ground covered with osage orange hedge trees, sporting from four to eight inch thorns. Neither of us had been awake enough to realize my predicament. Broken branches lay everywhere. I was wearing tennis shoes, and I had one flashlight and a very sick horse to get home. I put Ginger in the corral behind the house at 3 a.m.

At daybreak, I was back out looking. I found the other horses, standing in a corner of the neighbor's pasture. Butterball had a corn stalk driven about five inches into her shoulder. The Tennessee Walker, Black Beauty, had a big triangular tear in her leg and shoulder. I called the vet. His wife said, "Bill is trying to get a Shetland pony loose that is trapped in a ball of woven wire fence. I will send him out when he finishes." Our four party phone had worked up until that phone call and then no more. Our electricity had been out since right after the tornado passed.

From Martin City, the tornado had gone on through Ruskin Heights wreaking extensive damages. It had traveled 71 miles on the ground and varied in width from one half to three miles.

Kansas City Star article on the tornado

On May 20, 1957, a killer storm was born near Williamsburg, Kan. Its 71-mile path included Spring Hill, Martin City and Ruskin Heights.

Nature, swift and deadly

Twister tore apart land and lives

The cost

Dead: 44*   Injured: 531

Damaged or destroyed: Ruskin High School, Ruskin Junior High School, Ruskin Heights Shopping Center, businesses, churches and about 900 homes.

*as recorded in the authoritative significant tornadoes by Tom Grazulis; other tallies put the death toll at 46.

By BRIAN BURNES
Staff Writer

Forty years ago Tuesday, Helen Boyles and Audrey Beckley emerged from the same basement window on East 110th Street.

"My husband told me not to look," Boyles said. "But, of course, I had to."

"Like Lot's wife," said Beckley.

The scene, after Kansas City's

deadliest tornado roared through their Ruskin Heights neighborhood, proved accordingly biblical.

Trees stood stripped of spring foliage.

The Boyles family car occupied their former dining room, its four tires in the air. The home was obliterated, except for a concrete slab, plumbing pipes and a geyser of tapwater.

That was just one example of the power of the tornado, which

arrived in the early evening of May 20, 1957.

Boyles and Beckley were young mothers in Ruskin Heights then. Their homes were among more than 600 damaged or destroyed in the new subdivision in what is now south Kansas City.

Forty years later, they still live across from each other on East 110th Street. Together, they lived through those traumatic

See **RUSKIN, A-24,** Col. 1

Fleeing was survival — barely

By JIM SULLINGER
Staff Writer

The setting sun painted a spectacular reddish hue on the bottom of the clouds, but that's not what kept my younger brother and me at the kitchen window.

This fluffy batch of vapor slowly moved in a circular pattern on the horizon. The southerly spring wind was warm and humid, and gray clouds gathered in the west.

"Looks like we could get a little rain later," my father said as he left the dinner table for his favorite chair and the newspaper. It was about 6 p.m., May 20, 1957.

I had just turned 13, and we lived just south of Ottawa, Kan., on a large hill, with a drive-in theater and a truck stop as neighbors.

Usually, my brother, Robert, and I joined our parents in the living room after dinner. But this day was

See **FLEEING, A-25,** Col. 1

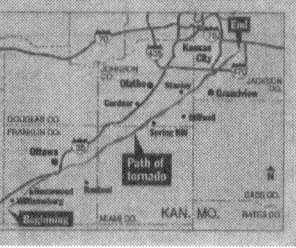

17

FARM REMINISCENCES

O children think about the
Good times

—Lucille Clifton (1936b.)

Mary Bob and I decided to move to the farm in 1955; we designed a French Mansard house with five different levels. The lowest level was the basement, the next contained a large family room with my office, a laundry, and a guest bath off it, then up to a living room, dining room, and kitchen area, up again to two bedrooms and two baths, and finally up to two more bedrooms. Kyger and Phyllis had the two top rooms with Kyger's being at the very back. Kyger was three when we moved to the farm. Barbara had just finished sixth grade. Barbara would start seventh grade at Stanley, but then transfer at semesters to Hilltop School just four miles down 175th Street. Hilltop had two classes in a room. The teacher would alternate between classes, having one class do paperwork, while presenting the other class lesson. Then he would move back to the other side of the class. There were seven in the seventh grade class and six in the eighth grade. Phyllis and Kyger attended Hilltop too with the class situation the same for a total of 4 classrooms, a kindergarten room, and a gymnasium.

One Christmas morning when Kyger was about five, the girls had tucked Kyger up against the wall in Phyllis' bed, so he wouldn't fall out. Mary Bob and I could hear them; they were hoping it would be time to get up soon and see if "Santa" had come. They had to wait until Mary Bob and I told them we were awake and then they could get up. That morning I slipped down and turned on the Christmas tree lights. This year I decided to shake some sleigh bells. When Kyger heard those bells, he hurdled his sisters and flew down the stairs right past me. He swore he saw Santa.

We were always having cattle troubles. We had one little heifer that could find any weak place in the fence. When I would go down to get her in, she would climb back in the way she got out. As soon as I would fix that place, she would find another.

One reason we decided to move to the farm was because someone had killed and butchered a couple of our calves. Another was the constant care the animals demanded. Our Hereford calves kept getting pink eye. When I switched to Angus, we had a 500 pound calf get out on the road one dark night and get killed.

We had a little bull calf born that had deformed front legs. He walked on his knees. I was going to dispose of him, but Aimee said that he would get along and make good eating. Phyl and Kyger loved him and named him Bucky. Barbara was in college. His mother would go off and leave him and come back maybe twice a day, so he could nurse. When Bucky got older, we had him butchered. He had never been able to move around much and was very tender. The major problem we had with raising our own eating animals was that the kids did not like eating steaks called "Bucky" or chickens called, "Crower."

Crower was a really mean rooster that someone had given us as a castoff Easter chick. In those day, the drug stores sold baby ducks and chicks whose plumage was dyed pink, blue, orange, or greens as Easter pets. Crower would fly down from the rafters of our horse barn and attack the kids whenever he liked. One night, I pronounced, "It is time we have Crower for dinner." The girls actually cheered. We all snuck down to the new horse barn in the dark. I caught Crower by the neck while he was asleep. With one swift twist of my hands, he was gone. And so were all three kids, fleeing in horror and tears, from his final death dance. We found a necklace charm of Barbara Lu's in his gizzard when we cleaned him.

I had had a lot of bad luck with my horses. I purchased a little stallion quarter horse colt and had him trained to race. Terrybars loved racing and was quite fast. Just before his first official race, he was practicing on his own and slipped. His foot went under the gate and he tore off his hoof. His racing days were ended. Shortly after, I bought a fine stud colt named Flying Jag that I also trained to race. The horse pen had steel rods and when lightening struck Jag was killed.

I got the idea that I wanted to learn to rope. I bought eight Brahma heifer calves about six months old from a place in Louisiana. In their first Kansas winter, they all caught pneumonia. We even brought some of them into the garage trying to save them. At the end of the winter, I only had two left and they were as different as day and night. One was a nice, big Brahma cow, a good looking animal. The other one was small and looked more like a billy goat than a cow. We named it "Stupid." Stupid caused us all kinds of problems, but she raised a good calf. The big Brahma had her first calf and her teats were so swollen that the calf couldn't get them in his mouth. He couldn't eat and soon caught pneumonia. We loaded him up in the back of the pickup and let the Brahma follow us home. Our farmer Aimee said the calf would never make it. Aimee had me buy a Holstein bull calf and put it on her. Phyllis, however, made me get the vet for the other calf. He gave Phyl some medicine and careful instructions for hand feeding it. In two weeks, that little calf was fine. His mother, though, was on a vendetta. She knew Phyllis had her calf. Any time she could, she would go after Phyllis.

We learned to vaccinate our cattle and to castrate the little bull calves, which helped to keep our vet bills down. Phyllis and I were outdoors a lot. She was my buddy and helper. We had to pull some new born calves. We also had to pull some foals, but I always had a vet present for the horses. We had two good looking registered Angus heifers born on March 10th one year. One was born in the morning and one later in the day. The temperature was about 10 degrees in the morning and warmed up some during the day. The first calf born had most of her ears frozen off and only about 6 inches of her tail left. She was a little odd looking, but she was a nice animal. We named her Short Tail. One day when Short Tail was about a year old, we were vaccinating all of the heifers for black leg. We would run them into the holding chute, catch them by the heads, give them a shot, and then release them. Not all of them wanted to cooperate, so Phyllis would climb up the side of the chute, grab the tails of the "noncooperatives" and twist them. These calves would try to get away from her and poke their heads in the trap. Then we would have them. We got Short Tail in the chute, but she wouldn't cooperate, so up Phyl goes and starts to twist this 6" stub. Whoops, off it came! Phyl turned a bit green, holding that little stub, but No Tail, formerly Short Tail, got her shots.

We decided that we were going to send the big Brahma's first calf down to Aimee's to fatten up and butcher. He was over a year old by this time. We got him in the truck and Aimee started off for his house 3/4 mile west of us. Aimee was almost home, when this steer decided to jump out of the truck and head north, going through fences at will. I guess he had his own suspicions about that truck ride. Aimee got some of his family and started out to head this little Brahma off, but the steer just disappeared. Reports of a Brahma steer came from as far as four miles away, but he couldn't be found.

My son Kyger (B.K.) stands outside our farm home with Lady, one of our dogs.

18

SNOW, DEEP SNOW

He will not see me stopping here
To watch his woods fill up with snow.

—**Robert Frost (1874–1963)**

I remember a really bad snow storm. Barbara told me that the snow started coming down about 3 p.m. and increased in velocity as the Spring Hill High School bus slowly navigated the country roads, depositing students at their rural homes. The Brooks home was the farthest on the route, but Mr. Mayes, the driver, was confident the bus could make it as the roads were paved there. "It's cold on this bus," Barbara said, as she moved up to the front and crowded next to the big heater that comforted the driver. The last high school student besides Barbara jumped off the bus into the rapidly rising drifts. "Bye, Penny," Barbara called as Penny ran up the driveway to the Renner residence. "See you tomorrow."

Mr. Mayes turned north and the bus crawled onto the paved road, now 175th Street. He turned west and continued the steady creep towards his final dropoff. It was nearly five p.m. and growing dark. The snow was wet and clumping on the windshield wipers. At the top of the Verhaeghe hill, the bus just stopped. Like a belligerent mule, it refused to go farther. Mr. Mayes rocked the bus' wheels, trying to unlock them from the slushy drifts that clung tightly and resisted any motion. Finally he gave up, "Bundle up, Barbara, we are going to have to walk up to Aimee's house and see if he can help us out."

Aime's white frame house could still be seen through the heavy white flakes. His wife Bertha opened the door to the knocking and welcomed the two ice coated travelers. "Aimee has just taken the tractor down to pick up your sister, Barbara," Bertha smiled. "The Hilltop bus was able to get her home. When she gets here, we will try to find the rest of your family."

By the time Aimee returned, the bus was firmly stuck. Bertha just laughed, "Well, looks like we will expand the chicken and noodles a bit and you all will spend the night here." Phyllis and I thought that sounded like a lot of fun. Bertha and Aime had a woodburning stove and their upper floors weren't heated, so we knew would be really bundled up. Our mother had called Phyllis. She and Kyger were stuck trying to come home from Olathe where he had had a doctor's appointment. They would spend the night with another hospitable farm family.

"Brrrrring, Brrrrring," went Aimee's phone. "That's our ring," cried Phyllis elatedly. "Maybe it's Dad." We were on a four party system, and each family answered just their ring (unless they were an eavesdropper!) This time, though, Bertha answered the Brooks' ring.

"Hi, Bertha," I stammered, a bit surprised by her voice. "I'm in Stanley. I followed the snow plows out, but I don't think I can make it in."

"Don't worry, Bert," said Bertha. "We have the girls here and Mary Bob and Kyger are with neighbors five miles north. Aimee fed your animals when he was down to get Phil."

"Okay, then I think I will try to get back to Kansas City and spend the night with Mary Bob's folks. The snowplows are clearing Highway 69 pretty regularly. I will follow one."

Kansas snowstorms often made travel difficult. My boss at the Marley Company was always "chewing" on somebody. I didn't let him have much of my hide. Once he left town and said, "Bert, you need to check the supplies at the Kansas Plant at the end of the week." A heavy snow storm blew in that Thursday. The employees were all let off early and I headed for home. I didn't even consider going to North Kansas City. When my boss got back Monday, he was furious and started in on me. He would just keep at an employee until the employee admitted guilt. I didn't feel guilty.

Sometimes he just wanted the employee to quit. He had called me once from the Louisville, Kentucky plant where they were trying to pass their mistakes off on me. I told him if he wanted to believe them then I would just clean out my desk. If he didn't want me there, then I was ready to leave. I hung up and started collecting my things. "Ring, ring," went the phone. "Bert, I'm sorry. I was just angry," my boss went on offering apologies. I was ready to leave that day. I felt I did what was right and others should respect me.

So shortly after I had failed to go to the Kansas Plant, I was supposed to fly out on Sunday afternoon to the Louisville plant. Snow started falling Saturday evening, continuing into Sunday, getting heavier all of the time. The east-west road in front of the house was starting to drift shut. I had our tractor out and was blading off the path to the barn so the kids could feed the horses. Then I bladed off the drive so I could get packed and go. The road was starting to drift shut in front of the house, but I was pretty sure I could make it to the north-south road a quarter mile down. But just as I was leaving, a car slid across the east-west road and blocked the entire path. I couldn't get this driver out. He came on down to the house with me and called for help.

Now I had to get out to the west. I changed clothes and got to the top of Aimee's hill. A huge drift covered the road. I was so mad I just gunned my big Chrysler coupe and hit that drift going full speed. The car lights went out and I came to a complete halt. I couldn't get the door open, so I rolled down the window and climbed on top of the car. Aimee had seen the whole fiasco and tried to drag me out with his tractor. So did a passerby in a jeep. Finally a road grader came down a side road. He stopped. "You need a longer chain," he hollered down at us. I got in with him and he dropped me off back at my driveway.

Mary Bob was glad to see me, "The airline called and cancelled your flight just after you left." So I went back up the drive. The road grader had come back with a longer chain and drug my car off to the side of the road, as well as the other man's car. Aimee helped me drag my car home. Snow was packed to the hood. My coupe was like a block of ice. I had to have a wrecker come get it the next day, but my boss didn't say anything about my not getting to Louisville.

19

SEARCHING FOR MY FATHER

What did I know, what did I know
Of love's austere and lonely offices?

—**Robert Hayden (1913–1980)**

Sometimes children are left to ponder family puzzle pieces. By the time the children care about the puzzle's picture, many of the pieces have been lost to death or decline. I am one of those children; I was born July 17, 1944, in Kansas City, Missouri, to Bert and Mary Roberta (Bob) Brooks. My father Bert wrote evocative and somewhat humorous memoirs of his life during his last years. He often portrays himself as a rather comical figure. He will comment, "I was probably the last kid in the neighborhood to wear long pants, a badge of distinction for my generation. I can remember going down to get a suit, certain I would have long pants, but my mother bought me one with knickers instead. The first time I wore it, I immediately fell down on the driveway and ripped the knee out of it. Mother cut the knees off and made shorts out of my knickers. Knees were cheaper than suit pants in those days. My long pants were postponed for another two years." My father describes himself as uncoordinated, "With thick glasses at age twelve, I hit a growth spurt that would leave me at age sixteen 6'2" tall and 130 pounds, a skinny, uncoordinated boy-man."

Most of his stories are about his boyhood and his war years, stories that I had never heard. My father loved his mother (Gram to me) dearly. When he died March 29, 2001, he dedicated a Reflection Garden at Menorah Medical Center, 5721 West 119th, Overland Park, Kansas, naming his mother, his doctor Mark C. Myron, the Menorah staff, and his WWII comrades as those in his thoughts. My sister Phyllis sold a large diamond ring that dad felt had caused sorrow and dissension in his family to fund the garden. He said Gram always loved gardening and she might appreciate this use of the funds from the ring.

We would visit Gram when I was small. She was a tall, regal woman, who always smiled. Her skin was mottled with brown age spots that fascinated me, and she wore coke-bottle glasses from the glaucoma that slowly stole her sight over twenty years. She would write to me my freshman year of college, always saying, "I love you" several times in the letter. I have her turquoise necklaces and some of her furniture. Jack, my husband, and I were fortunate enough to have two grandmothers at our wedding November 18, 1967: Gram and his maternal grandmother Olga Morehead.

My Aunt Phyllis, Gram's eldest daughter, lived with her. Phyllis was an alcoholic, heavyset, and always in a bathrobe when I knew her. My father told me, "She couldn't marry her first love. My father interfered, so she married Jim Adkinson after college. She was an interior designer and very talented, but when he came back from the war, Jim left her. She just gave up." Phyllis was always a shadow figure for me. Dad would say over and over to us kids, "Be careful of drinking. You can ruin your life." To me, Aunt Phyllis was living poster proof. Her picture on the black grand piano in Gram's living room showed a stunning, younger woman, totally unlike the sad, slow figure who frequented the upper rooms of Gram's home. I didn't have a drink until I graduated from college.

Gram's house was in Oklahoma City on 2115 N.W. 18th Street. It was a two story brick with a screened-in porch, a detached garage, and a big pecan tree in the back yard. Her mother Katie Vashti Orr (9/2/1868–2/15/1952) also lived with her. We didn't visit Gram a lot because my mother didn't like her. My mother said, "Gram talked Bert into enlisting. She wanted him to get back in good with his old man." My mother and Gram had an ongoing feud. When my mother complained about my father's quietness, Gram told her, "It's because you always talk over him, Mary Bob." Gram, Aunt Phyllis, and Great-Grandmother Orr are all buried in Memorial Park Cemetery in Okalahoma City.

My mother would tell me, "I walked the tires off the 'tailor tot' with you," meaning the metal stroller of the 1940's. Then she would say, "You were my life, Barbara Lu." After my parents bought the house at 4006 West 69th Street in Prairie Village, she emphasized, "You would scream and lay on the floor, yelling 'I don't want Daddy anymore,' because I was too busy making dinner. You would turn blue with rage."

I don't remember that. I do remember my father's last days in the hospital when the nurses put white elastic bands on his legs that looked like long hose. He was embarrassed. Yet dressed in that hospital nightgown, he put his arms around

Mom and me. We sat in the window bench of the hospital room that dreary March 2001 and laughed at his attire and celebrated the joy of being together. My daughter Chris and my grandson Cameron John born in March the previous year had come with me to see him. Sadness was sweetened with the presence of a new generation.

Chris now has a little boy Jack Ryan that has the exact dimples my father had—one in the back of each shoulder. Dad told me that he was shot in one shoulder during the war and the bullet came out the other. That's a story I can't believe anymore, but most of these stories, I believe. Understanding another person is difficult, and although I still have many questions, stories do bring substance. I now must write my own stories.

Bert Jr.'s great grandsons, Cameron John and Jack Ryan Collins, share their wonderful smiles and zest for life. May their flowers grow freely, their brooks run clearly and rapidly, and any cloudy days turn to golden sunsets.

BERT BROOKS SR. MATERNAL LINEAGE

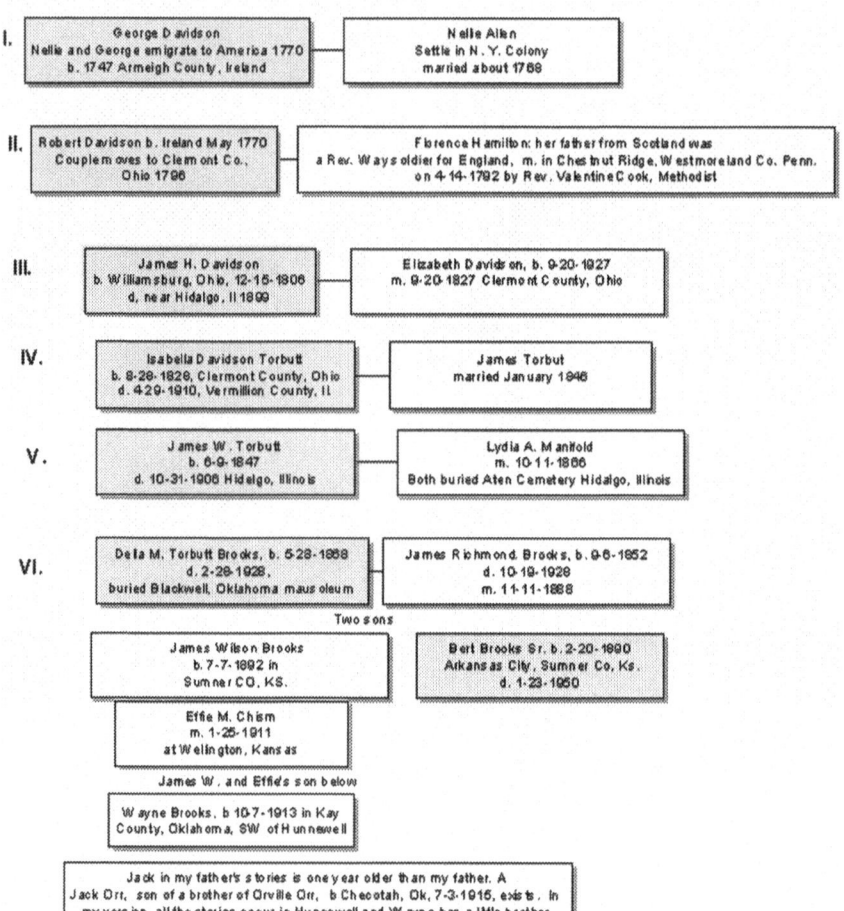

I.
George Davidson
Nellie and George emigrate to America 1770
b. 1747 Armeigh County, Ireland

Nellie Allen
Settle in N.Y. Colony
married about 1768

II.
Robert Davidson b. Ireland May 1770
Couple moves to Clermont Co.,
Ohio 1796

Florence Hamilton: her father from Scotland was
a Rev. Way soldier for England, m. in Chestnut Ridge, Westmoreland Co. Penn.
on 4-14-1792 by Rev. Valentine Cook, Methodist

III.
James H. Davidson
b. Williamsburg, Ohio, 12-15-1906
d. near Hidalgo, Il 1869

Elizabeth Davidson, b. 9-20-1927
m. 9-20-1827 Clermont County, Ohio

IV.
Isabella Davidson Torbutt
b. 8-28-1826, Clermont County, Ohio
d. 4-29-1910, Vermillion County, Il

James Torbut
married January 1846

V.
James W. Torbutt
b. 6-9-1847
d. 10-31-1906 Hidalgo, Illinois

Lydia A. Manifold
m. 10-11-1866
Both buried Aten Cemetery Hidalgo, Ilinois

VI.
Dela M. Torbutt Brooks, b. 5-28-1868
d. 2-28-1928,
buried Blackwell, Oklahoma mausoleum

James Richmond Brooks, b. 9-6-1852
d. 10-19-1928
m. 11-11-1888

Two sons

James Wilson Brooks
b. 7-7-1892 in
Sumner CO, KS.

Bert Brooks Sr. b. 2-20-1890
Arkansas City, Sumner Co, Ks.
d. 1-23-1950

Effie M. Chism
m. 1-25-1911
at Welington, Kansas

James W. and Effie's son below

Wayne Brooks, b 10-7-1913 in Kay
County, Oklahoma, SW of Hunnewell

Jack in my father's stories is one year older than my father. A
Jack Orr, son of a brother of Orville Orr, b Checotah, Ok, 7-3-1915, exists. In
my version, all the stories occur in Hunnewell and Wayne has a little brother.

BERT BROOKS SR. PATERNAL FAMILY LINEAGE

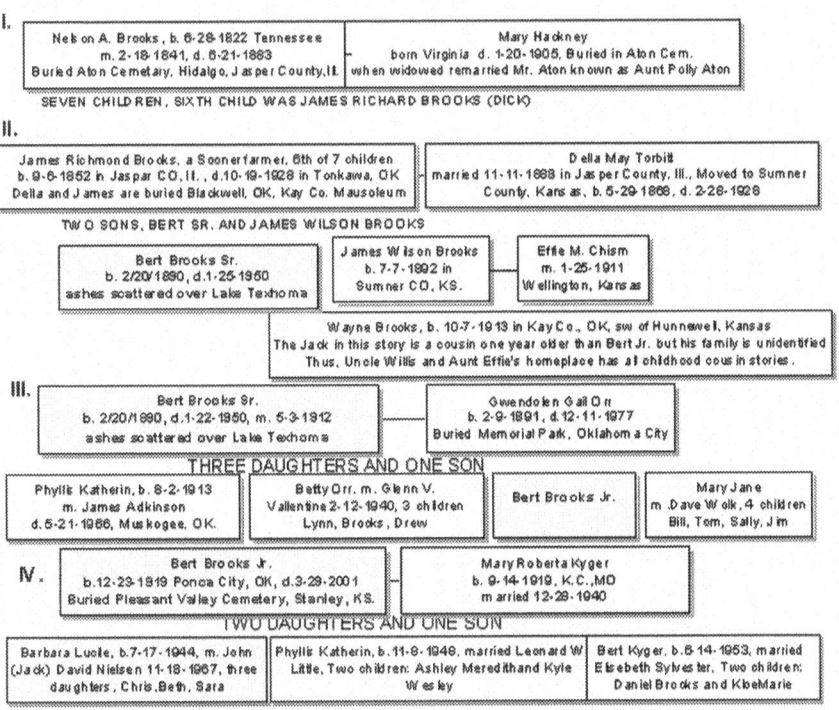

I.

| Nelson A. Brooks, b. 6-28-1822 Tennessee
m. 2-18-1841, d. 6-21-1883
Buried Aton Cemetary, Hidalgo, Jasper County, Ill. | Mary Hackney
born Virginia d. 1-20-1905, Buried in Aton Cem.
when widowed remarried Mr. Aton known as Aunt Polly Aton |

SEVEN CHILDREN, SIXTH CHILD WAS JAMES RICHARD BROOKS (DICK)

II.

| James Richmond Brooks, a Sooner farmer, 6th of 7 children
b. 9-6-1852 in Jaspar CO, Ill., d.10-19-1928 in Tonkawa, OK
Della and James are buried Blackwell, OK, Kay Co. Mausoleum | Della May Torbitt
married 11-11-1888 in Jasper County, Ill., Moved to Sumner
County, Kansas, b. 5-29-1868, d. 2-28-1928 |

TWO SONS, BERT SR. AND JAMES WILSON BROOKS

| Bert Brooks Sr.
b. 2/20/1890, d.1-25-1950
ashes scattered over Lake Texhoma | James Wilson Brooks
b. 7-7-1892 in
Sumner CO, KS. | Effie M. Chism
m. 1-25-1911
Wellington, Kansas |

Wayne Brooks, b. 10-7-1913 in Kay Co., OK, sw of Hunnewell, Kansas
The Jack in this story is a cousin one year older than Bert Jr. but his family is unidentified
Thus, Uncle Willis and Aunt Effie's homeplace has all childhood cousin stories.

III.

| Bert Brooks Sr.
b. 2/20-1890, d.1-22-1950, m. 5-3-1912
ashes scattered over Lake Texhoma | Gwendolen Gail Orr
b. 2-9-1891, d. 12-11-1977
Buried Memorial Park, Oklahoma City |

THREE DAUGHTERS AND ONE SON

| Phyllis Katherin, b. 8-2-1913
m. James Adkinson
d. 5-21-1986, Muskogee, OK. | Betty Orr, m. Glenn V.
Vallentine 2-12-1940, 3 children
Lynn, Brooks, Drew | Bert Brooks Jr. | Mary Jane
m .Dave Wolk, 4 children
Bill, Tom, Sally, Jim |

IV.

| Bert Brooks Jr.
b.12-23-1919 Ponca City, OK, d.3-29-2001
Buried Pleasant Valley Cemetery, Stanley, KS. | Mary Roberta Kyger
b. 9-14-1919, K.C.,MO
married 12-28-1940 |

TWO DAUGHTERS AND ONE SON

| Barbara Lucile, b.7-17-1944, m. John
(Jack) David Nielsen 11-18-1967, three
daughters, Chris,Beth, Sara | Phyllis Katherin, b. 11-8-1948, married Leonard W
Little, Two children: Ashley Meredith and Kyle
Wesley | Bert Kyger, b.8-14-1953, married
Elisabeth Sylvester, Two children:
Daniel Brooks and KloeMarie |

EACH OF THESE THREE CHILDREN HAS THEIR OWN PAGE.

GWENDOLEN GAEL **ORR** PATERNAL LINEAGE

I.

| William Orr, b. Clare County, Ireland, emigrated 1763 to Northumberland Co., Penn. Died in Kentucky 1791, d. Bourbon, Co, Ky. Has 3 sons William, Joseph, Grayson | No record but William is the 1st son, and Joseph the 2nd |

II.

| William Vernon Orr, Justice of the Peace, b. Northumberland Co., Penn. 3-18-1775, d. 3-28-1875 Lima, Adams Co., Ill. | Elizabeth Turner, b. Frankfort, Ky, 2-1-1788, William operates first mill in Lima. He and brother Joseph lay out and name Lima. |

III.

| Thomas Grayson Orr, b. Bourbon Co, KY, 2-6-1810, d. Adams Co, Il 12-14-1887, buried Orr Cemetary, Lima, farmed | Mary Jane Wood, b. 2-9-1820, d. 6-13-1896 |

IV.

| Oscar Orr, b 10-16-1839, Lima, d. Putnam Co., Mo 9-18, 1865, First child | Louise/Louisa Lemmon, b. Adams Co, Ill. 12-20-1839, d. Chillicothe, Mo. 10-30-1909 buried Ursa, Adams Co, Ill |

V.

| Orville Orr, b. 10-24-1867 Ursa, Adams Co, Ill., d. 9-21-1896, buried Keith Cem, Ursa | Katie Vashti Dunham b.9-2-1868, d. Oklahoma City, OK 2-15-1952 |

See Dunham Page for Additional Ancestry.

VI.

| Gwendolen Gael Orr b. Wheeling, Mo. 2-9-1891, lived in Muskogee, and Oklahoma City | Bert Brooks Sr. m. Frederick, Tillman Co, OK 5-3-1912 |

Gwendolen Gael DUNHAM Orr Brooks Maternal Lineage

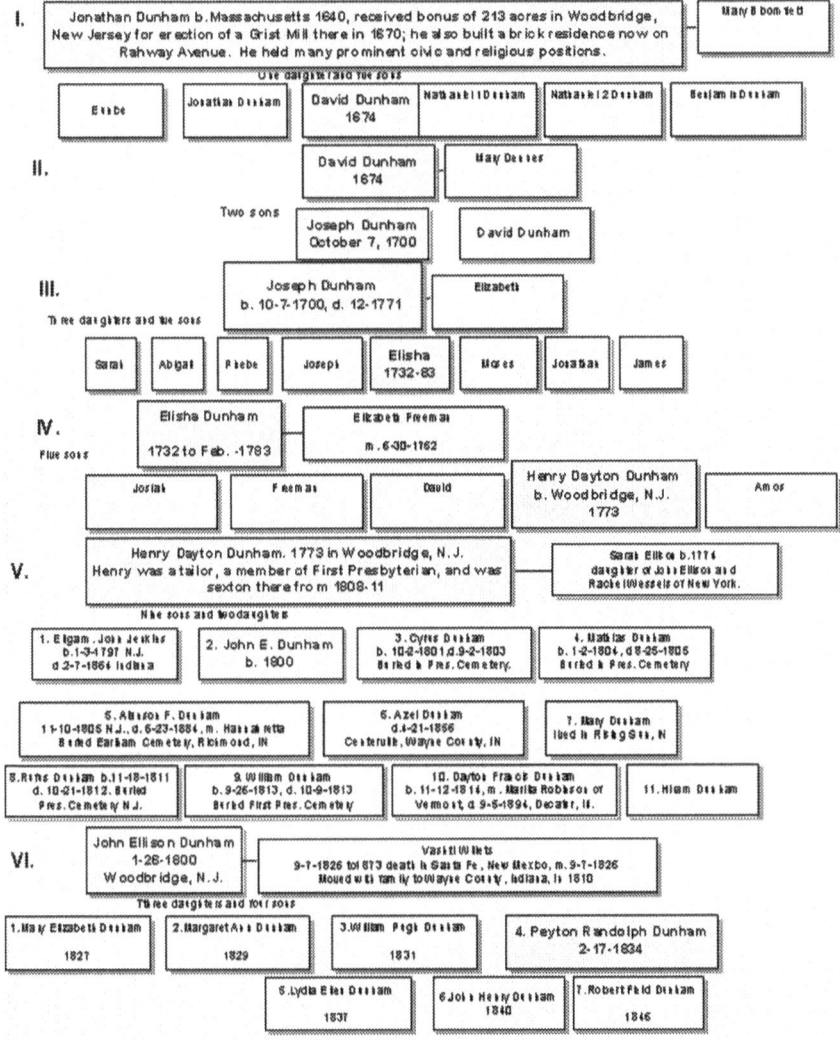

I. Jonathan Dunham b. Massachusetts 1640, received bonus of 213 acres in Woodbridge, New Jersey for erection of a Grist Mill there in 1670; he also built a brick residence now on Rahway Avenue. He held many prominent civic and religious positions.

Mary B born 1641

One daughter and five sons

| Eliabe | Jonathan Dunham | David Dunham 1674 | Nathaniel 1 Dunham | Nathaniel 2 Dunham | Benjamin Dunham |

II. David Dunham 1674 — Mary Dennes

Two sons

Joseph Dunham October 7, 1700 — David Dunham

III. Joseph Dunham b. 10-7-1700, d. 12-1771 — Elizabeth

Three daughters and five sons

| Sarah | Abigail | Phebe | Joseph | Elisha 1732-83 | Moses | Jonathan | James |

IV. Elisha Dunham 1732 to Feb. -1783 — Elizabeth Freeman m. 6-30-1762

Five sons

| Josiah | Freeman | David | Henry Dayton Dunham b. Woodbridge, N.J. 1773 | Amos |

V. Henry Dayton Dunham. 1773 in Woodbridge, N.J. Henry was a tailor, a member of First Presbyterian, and was sexton there from 1808-11 — Sarah Ellison b.1774 daughter of John Ellison and Rachel Wessels of New York.

Nine sons and two daughters

| 1. Elgam. John Jenkins b.1-3-1797 N.J. d.2-7-1866 Indiana | 2. John E. Dunham b. 1800 | 3. Cyrus Dunham b. 10-2-1801,d.9-2-1803 Buried h Pres. Cemetery. | 4. Mathias Dunham b.1-2-1804, d 8-25-1805 Buried h Pres. Cemetery |

| 5. Abraham F. Dunham 1-10-1805 N.J., d.6-23-1884, m. Hannah retta Buried Earlham Cemetery, Richmond, IN | 6. Azel Dunham d.4-21-1856 Centerville, Wayne County, IN | 7. Mary Dunham lived in Rising Sun, N |

| 8. Rufus Dunham b.11-18-1811 d. 10-21-1812. Buried Pres. Cemetery N.J. | 9. William Dunham b.9-26-1813, d. 10-9-1813 Buried First Pres. Cemetery | 10. Dayton Franch Dunham b. 11-12-1816, m. Martha Robison of Vermont, d 9-5-1894, Decatur, Il. | 11. Hiram Dunham |

VI. John Ellison Dunham 1-26-1800 Woodbridge, N.J. — Vashti Willets 9-7-1826 to 1813 death h Santa Fe, New Mexbo, m. 9-7-1826 Moved with family to Wayne County, Indiana, in 1810

Three daughters and four sons

| 1.Mary Elizabeth Dunham 1827 | 2.Margaret Ann Dunham 1829 | 3.William Pugh Dunham 1831 | 4. Peyton Randolph Dunham 2-17-1834 |

| 5.Lydia Ellen Dunham 1837 | 6.John Henry Dunham 1840 | 7.Robert Field Dunham 1846 |

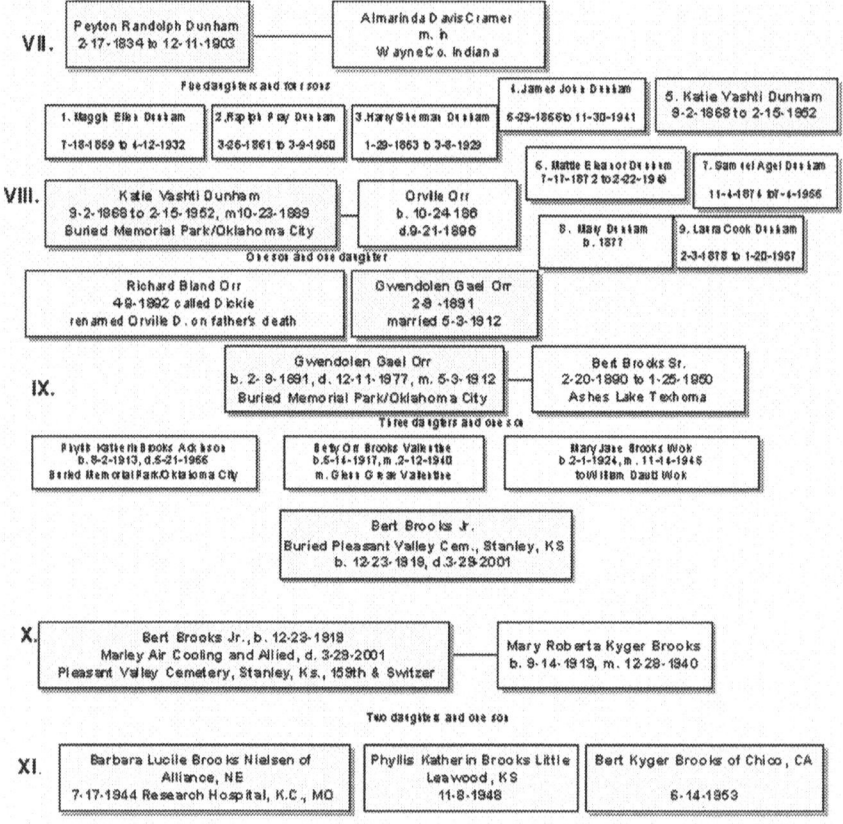

VII.

Peyton Randolph Dunham
2-17-1834 to 12-11-1903

Almarinda Davis Cramer
m. in
Wayne Co. Indiana

Five daughters and four sons

1. Maggie Ella Dunham
7-18-1859 to 4-12-1932

2. Ralph Ray Dunham
3-26-1861 to 3-9-1950

3. Mary Sherman Dunham
1-29-1863 b 3-8-1929

4. James John Dunham
6-29-1866 to 11-30-1941

5. Katie Vashti Dunham
9-2-1868 to 2-15-1952

6. Mattie Eleanor Dunham
7-17-1872 to 2-22-1948

7. Samuel Agel Dunham
11-4-1874 to 7-4-1955

VIII.

Katie Vashti Dunham
9-2-1868 to 2-15-1952, m10-23-1889
Buried Memorial Park/Oklahoma City

Orville Orr
b. 10-24-186
d.9-21-1896

8. May Dunham
b. 1877

9. Laura Cook Dunham
2-3-1878 to 1-20-1967

One son and one daughter

Richard Bland Orr
4-9-1892 called Dickie
renamed Orville D. on father's death

Gwendolen Gael Orr
2-9-1891
married 5-3-1912

IX.

Gwendolen Gael Orr
b. 2-9-1891, d. 12-11-1977, m. 5-3-1912
Buried Memorial Park/Oklahoma City

Bert Brooks Sr.
2-20-1890 to 1-25-1950
Ashes Lake Texhoma

Three daughters and one son

Phyllis Katherine Brooks Adkisson
b. 8-2-1913, d. 5-21-1966
Buried Memorial Park/Oklahoma City

Betty Orr Brooks Valkentine
b. 5-14-1917, m. 2-12-1940
m. Glen Grace Valkentine

Mary Jane Brooks Wiok
b 2-1-1924, m. 11-4-1945
to William David Wiok

Bert Brooks Jr.
Buried Pleasant Valley Cem., Stanley, KS
b. 12-23-1919, d. 3-29-2001

X.

Bert Brooks Jr., b. 12-23-1919
Marley Air Cooling and Allied, d. 3-29-2001
Pleasant Valley Cemetery, Stanley, Ks., 159th & Switzer

Mary Roberta Kyger Brooks
b. 9-14-1919, m. 12-28-1940

Two daughters and one son

XI.

Barbara Lucile Brooks Nielsen of
Alliance, NE
7-17-1944 Research Hospital, K.C., MO

Phyllis Katherin Brooks Little
Leawood, KS
11-8-1948

Bert Kyger Brooks of Chico, CA

6-14-1953

See following pages for descendents of Bert and Mary Bob Brooks' three children.

Pictures of first Dunham home in United States. The Jonathan Dunham homestead still stands and one of his original millstones has been placed on a concrete base in the circular drive opposite the entrance to the dwelling. Alongside it, the Township of Woodbridge dedicated a monument on October 5, 1969, during the 300th anniversary of Woodbridge. Jonathan Dunham was one of its first citizens and a most distinguished individual. On June 8, 1970, he was cited in the Congressional Record and by the New Jersey State Senate. In 1701 he served as a delegate to the Assembly, sitting in Elizabethtown. New Jersey. (Quoted from a letter written by Lester Robert Dunham on December 12, 1970.

FAMILY LINEAGE CONTINUED FOR CHILDREN OF MARY BOB AND BERT BROOKS

BARBARA AND JACK NIELSEN

Barbara Lucile Brooks Nielsen, Ph.D. English 7-17-1944, Research Hospital, Kansas City, MO m. 11-18-1967, Prairie Village	John David (Jack) Nielsen, b. 3-10-1939, St. Joseph Hospital Alliance, NE IBM ten years, Diamond Hill Farms

Dana Christine Nielsen 8-25-1970 Lincoln General, Lincoln, Ne	Elisebeth Ayn Nielsen b. 2-20-1973, Pasavant Hospital, Chicago, Illinois	Sara Alyss Nielsen b. 9-9-1974 Ft. Wayne, In.

I. First daughter of Barbara and Jack Nielsen

Dana Christine Nielsen Collin, b. 8-25-1970 m. 11-14-1997 Holy Rosary Church, IBM Program Mgr.	Michael Edward Collins, farmer b. 10-9-1969 Alliance, NE

Cameron John Collins 3-22-2000, Alliance, NE Box Butte Co Hospital		Jack Ryan Collins 7-2-2002, Alliance, NE Box Butte Co Hospital	

Second daughter of Barbara and Jack Nielsen

II.

Elisebeth Ayn Nielsen, b. 2-20-1973, Merck Pharmaceutical Rep. Dallas, Texas	

III. Third daughter of Barbara and Jack Nielsen

Sara Alyss Nielsen, b. 9-9-1974, Software Consultant, Denver, Colorado	

Sara Alyss Nielsen is standing by her middle sister Beth on the left and older sister Chris on the right. Their mother Barbara and father Jack are truly blessed with such lovely, caring, competent daughters.

FAMILY LINEAGE CONTINUED FOR CHILDREN OF MARY BOB AND BERT BROOKS

PHYLLIS K. AND LEONARD W. LITTLE

Phylis Katherin Brooks b. 11-8-1948, Kansas City, Mo. m. 4-19-1975, Leawood Kansas	Leonard W. Little

Daughter of Phyllis and Leonard W. Little

I.

Ashley Meredith Little, b. 12-29-1976	Eric Douglas Frankel, b. 8-27-1976, m. 4-3-2004 Jenner, CA.

II. Son of Phyllis and Leonard W. Little

Kyle Wesley Little, b. 11-23-79	

Leonard Little, his wife Phyllis, and their daughter Ashley and son Kyle appear in a family studio portrait. From her birth on, Phyllis has been a best friend, a confident, and a source of support to her older sister Barbara.

FAMILY LINEAGE CONTINUED FOR CHILDREN OF MARY BOB AND BERT BROOKS

B.K. (Bert Kyger)and Beth (Elizabeth) Brooks

Bert Kyger Brooks b. 6-14-1953, Kansas City, Missouri	Elizabeth Sylvester

I. Son of B.K. and Beth Brooks

Daniel Boone Brooks, b. 1-22-1993	

II. Daughter of B.K. and Beth Brooks

Kloe Marie Brooks b. 11-30-1995	

B.K. and Beth Brooks in the summer of 2000 at the Lake Texhoma family celebration of Bert and Mary Bob's 60th anniversary. Beth hugs Kloe Marie Brooks and B.K. holds Daniel Boone Brooks. B.K., the younger brother by nine years, has been blessed with a wonderful family barely a few years older than his sister Barbara's grandchildren.

978-0-595-35044-5
0-595-35044-5